OH, TO BE IN ENGLAND

T0353256

David Pinner

OH, TO BE IN ENGLAND

OBERON BOOKS
LONDON

First published in 2011 by Oberon Books Ltd
521 Caledonian Road, London N7 9RH
Tel: 020 7607 3637 / Fax: 020 7607 3629
e-mail: info@oberonbooks.com
www.oberonbooks.com

A catalogue record for this book is available from the British
Library.

ISBN: 978-1-84943-056-2

Cover design by James Illman

Characters

GEORGE HAMPTON

KAY HAMPTON
his wife

ROB HAMPTON
their son

ANTONIA ELKIND

FLORIAN GRUNEWALD

Oh, To Be In England was first performed at the Finborough Theatre, London on 9th January 2011 with the following cast:

GEORGE HAMPTON, Peter Broome

KAY HAMPTON, Charlotte Thornton

ROB HAMPTON, Daniel Fraser

ANTONIA ELKIND, Natalie Lesser

FLORIAN GRUNEWALD, Jonathan Christie

Director, Mel Cook

Assistant Director, Alex Barclay

Designer, Alison Neighbour

ACT ONE

SCENE ONE

St George's Day (April 23) 1974. Evening.

A comfortable lounge/dining room in Barnes, S.W.13, with doors leading to the kitchen, the hall and the garden. On the walls are reproductions of Turner, Gainsborough and Reynolds.

KAY HAMPTON, an attractive woman in her early Forties, is wearing a very paint-stained smock. Feverishly she is applying red paint to a canvas, which is propped up against the T.V. set. She seems nervous.

The front door bangs. KAY jumps. Quickly she collects her brushes and canvas. She rushes into the kitchen with them, shutting the door behind her.

ROBERT HAMPTON, who is KAY's eighteen-year-old son, enters. He is handsome and mature for his years, and he is wearing a battered school uniform, with a Prefect's insignia in his lapel.

KAY: *(Off.)* That you, darling?

ROB: *(Throwing his satchel down.)* No.

    (KAY comes in, without her paint smock.)

KAY: Oh. It's you, Rob.

ROB: Yes.

KAY: Have a good day?

ROB: No.

KAY: Oh.

ROB: What's that on your nose?

KAY: Flour.

ROB: It's red.

KAY: *(Quickly rubbing the red paint off her nose with her pinafore.)*
    Probably blood. Been chopping onions. Hope you're
    hungry.

ROB: No thanks, Mum. Had a bite after the debate.

KAY: Did you win?

ROB: No.

KAY: Oh. What was it about?

ROB: 'The pros and cons of the implementation of the Balfour Declaration.'

KAY: What's that when it's at home?

ROB: Depends which side you're on.

KAY: It's not like him to be late. *(Going into the kitchen.)* Dinner's ruined.

ROB: *(Sniffing.)* Isn't it!

KAY: Not like him. Always rings me.

ROB: Dad's been acting strangely recently, hasn't he?

KAY: *(Off.)* Suppose he has been a bit withdrawn.

(KAY comes back with a glass of milk and a packet of biscuits for ROB.)

ROB: Oh, you've noticed.

KAY: *(Nodding and eating a biscuit.)* You know how your Dad's always burbling on about his dreams of the 'ideal life'. Well, for the last couple of weeks he hasn't.

ROB: Perhaps they've been fulfilled.

KAY: I don't follow.

ROB: *(Peering into the garden.)* God, look at that moon.

KAY: Hope he hasn't told Lord Seagrove where to get off again.

ROB: I can't see what Dad sees in the Stock Market.

KAY: Don't make fun of him. He's worked very hard to get where he is.

ROB: Come and look at this moon.

KAY: What's so special about it?

(She joins him by the window.)

ROB: When I was cycling home, I kept looking up at it. Then I stared at those millions and millions of other suns and moons. In the face of all that, everything we do seems puerile. *(Pause)* You do know where Dad is, don't you?

KAY: No.

ROB: *(Mischievously.)* Fulfilling his dream.

KAY: *(Munching another biscuit.)* These are rather good.

ROB: With his mistress.

KAY: His....? *(Laughing.)* Don't be ridiculous!

ROB: I don't see anything ridiculous in Dad having a bit on the side.

KAY: That's quite enough, Rob, a joke's a joke but...

ROB: You mean he hasn't told you that he's been having a ding-dong with Antonia for the last three weeks?

KAY: *(Spitting out a mouthful of crumbs.)* Antonia!

ROB: Messy Mum.

(ROB goes into the hall.)

KAY: You do mean Mrs. Elkind?

ROB: *(Coming back with the carpet sweeper.)* Yes. Her with the frontage and the Degree from Trinity.

KAY: Oh, come on!

ROB: *(Sweeping up the crumbs.)* Wouldn't *you* sleep with her?

KAY: Me?

ROB: If you had the chance.

KAY: It's obvious *you've* been thinking about it.

ROB: True. But unfortunately Dad got in first.

KAY: Robert!

ROB: *(Putting the sweeper away.)* He's over there now.

KAY: You're not serious, are you?

ROB: What other explanation is there? If she wasn't entertaining him, she'd be over here now, wouldn't she?

KAY: Well...

ROB: Eight o'clock is her time to come round and borrow milk.

KAY: Yes, but...

ROB: And the tea to go with it.

KAY: It's unthinkable!

ROB: It was Tampax on Sunday.

KAY: Your Dad wouldn't have the nerve.

ROB: You'd think with what Steve earns, she could at least afford to buy her own Tampax.

KAY: Stop trying to shock me.

ROB: Thought I was being helpful.

KAY: I've seen him flirt with her, of course. But the idea of him, well, consummating his fatherly lust on the poor girl. Not a chance. He's too Puritan. And sadly much too English.

ROB: Sadly?

KAY: Yes. There's part of me wishes he could switch himself on and take an emotional risk. A few volts whizzing through him would perk us all up. It'd be quite exciting to get an electric shock every time we kissed. *(Pause.)* He's not really with her, is he? *(ROB grins, while KAY picks up a long crimson strip of her crochet work, and starts to crochet.)* I do wish he'd ring or something.

ROB: Would *you* like to have an affair?

KAY: *(Laughing.)* What a question.

ROB: You would!

KAY: With women, it's different.

ROB: What's different about it?

KAY: We tend to become absurdly involved. I wouldn't be able to help it. When you're older, it'll make more sense.

ROB: Have you ever... you know? *(KAY smiles.)* Does Dad know?

KAY: He knows as much as you do. And you seem to know more than both of us.

ROB: He doesn't, then.

KAY: *(Mischievous.)* We wouldn't want him to go berserk, would we?

ROB: *(Amused.)* You think he would?

KAY: You never know.

ROB: Dad on the rampage with a shotgun. Or his axe!

KAY: Or both.

ROB: Wouldn't that be terrific? Us splattered all over *The News of The World*!

KAY: Literally.

ROB: Yeah, I bet he's insanely jealous behind that grin.

KAY: We should've gone to the States when we had the chance. The Americans understand stocks and investment. But, oh, no, your father wouldn't take the risk of a new experience in a tough country. He was too busy giving Lord Seagrove advice, which, of course, his boss didn't take. Mind, Englishmen together are very worrying. I'd go tomorrow.

ROB: To America?

KAY: Anywhere. America. Dublin. Greece. Always wanted to go to Greece. With all that naked sunlight. *(Taking a book off the shelf.)* Look. Delphi. *(Showing him a photograph in the book.)* Isn't it naked?

ROB: Yeah, and so are half the men.

KAY: Sex isn't everything, dear. Not quite.

ROB: Do you sit flicking through these, when no one's here?

KAY: You can almost taste the olives. And that blue sky. The intense sweep of it. The white sand and even whiter stones, and no one there to intrude.

ROB: Except the Greeks. There's plenty of them.

KAY: I'm sure I'd get on very well with them. Extraordinarily well. It's the Dead that would trouble me. I'd be bound to feel Them in those derelict temples. In Greece the Dead are the Living. Every broken pillar is Agamemnon, or Achilles. Or Medea. I'd loved to have met Medea.

ROB: Why?

KAY: She cut through all restraints. There's a lot to be said for that.

ROB: Oh, Mum, you sound just like Dad. It's terrible.

KAY: *(Returning to her crochet.)* That's what happens.

ROB: Hm?

KAY: You become the person you marry. If you're not careful, you can lose your own personality entirely. The butcher offered to take me.

ROB: To Delphi?

KAY: Yes. I happened to mention I was born there.

ROB: Grandma said you were born in Southsea.

KAY: I was. But in one of my previous reincarnations I was born at Delphi. *(Crocheting.)* Never take up crochet, it destroys the soul.

ROB: Reincar...? Thought you were an Anglican?

KAY: I am. But as I grow older, I become more adaptable. Got him quite excited.

ROB: Who?

KAY: Grundy, the butcher. For the first time he cut all the fat off. Best chops we ever had.

ROB: Jesus! You and Dad must be appallingly miserable together.

KAY: *(Laughing.)* Nonsense. Your father and I are as happy as sandboys. He's the best husband in the world. Most of the time. Though, occasionally, I wish he'd whisk me off to the jungle or somewhere. We're dead such a long time.

(Pause.)

ROB: Mum?

KAY: Where the devil is he?

ROB: I didn't do well in my Mock.

KAY: *(Concerned.)* Really?

ROB: *(Handing her his results slip.)* Got an 'A' in English. But Geography and History were definitely iffy...

KAY: Your father'll be furious.

ROB: Yeah, I'm bound to get all that stuff about... *(In a cod Lancashire accent.)* ...'Grandfather down t'mines with his coal-dust sandwiches'. How Granddad slaved his guts out to give his son a good education, as his son in his turn has slaved *his* guts out down the mines of the Stock Exchange, to give his son an even better education, but *his* son has turned out to be a no-good idler, who can think of nothing but birds and booze.

KAY: Oh, don't be such a phoney!

ROB: What's the point, Mum? *(Picking up The Times.)* Everywhere you turn, it's hopeless. It must be. Even *The Times* has caught on. *(Reading.)* 'Students on vocation push up the total of jobless'. That's on Page One. Page Two; 'The University of Essex begins the most critical term of its history as student pickets again try to stop supplies being moved in'. So even if I did survive the collapse of the University system and managed to scrape a degree in English, what could I do after?

KAY: Well, you... There are lots of things.

ROB: No, English is such a bum subject. All you can do with English is to teach it to some other bums who, in turn, will get bum degrees in it, and teach it to even more bums. So it goes on; bums teaching bums ad infinitum.

KAY: There are still good schools to teach in.

ROB: *(Waving The Times at her.)* Not according to the MP for Fylde North.

KAY: Hm?

ROB: He's renewing his demand for 'A big enquiry into school vandalism, truancy and violence to teachers in the Comprehensive Sector.'

KAY: You're making it up.

ROB: Here, look. St. George's Day, April 23rd 1974. Column three, halfway down. Hey, hey! And take a butchers at Page 3.

KAY: Do I have to?

ROB: It's Dad!

KAY: What?

ROB: Yeah. At last he's made it in *The Times*.

KAY: Where?

(KAY grabs at the paper, but ROB escapes with it round the back of the sofa.)

ROB: *(Reading.)* 'Police raided a house on the outskirts of London yesterday afternoon, where they discovered a virtual Aladdin's Cave of obscene books and films.'

KAY: Let me see that!

ROB: *(Holding her at bay.)* '...The settings for these obscene films were fields and woods in Hertfordshire...'

KAY: That's where his secretary lives! Give it me!

ROB: '...Two men and three women took part in home movies called 'House of Mirrors', 'Kinky Capers', and 'Sex Mad Sisters', said Mr. Richard Du Cann for the Prosecution at St. Albans' Court yesterday.'

KAY: Where's it mention your father?

ROB: *The Times* is too genteel a paper to name names, Mum. That's why we take it. To prove we've made it into the Middle Class.

KAY: You've been having me on again.

ROB: Now would I kid you about Dad and our sexy neighbour, making 'Kinky Capers' in 'House of Mirrors' together? *(KAY swipes at him. ROB grabs her wrists. They struggle. He tickles her.)* You're not strong enough, Mumsy.

KAY: *(Laughing helplessly.)* Stop that, Rob, now stop it!

(They hear the back door. They break, still laughing.)

KAY: There he is! *(Calling out.)* George?

ROB: He must've just nipped back over Sexy's fence.

(Enter ANTONIA ELKIND (29), a beautiful, willowy woman.)

KAY: *(Under her breath.)* Ah… 'Sexy' herself.

ANTONIA: Who is?

KAY: My son was saying *you* were. *(Beaming.)* And, of course, you are.

ANTONIA: *(Unsure how to take it.)* Oh, thank you. Sorry, I didn't knock, Kay, but... well, you couldn't spare me a drop of milk and a large safety pin, could you?

KAY: I've got plenty of milk, Antonia, but unfortunately Robert's not needed to pin up his nappies since he went to the 'Big school'. Still, if he continues to get Mock A Level Results like he has today, I might have to buy him some new ones.

(KAY goes into the kitchen.)

ANTONIA: Sorry to barge in like this, Robert.

ROB: Don't be.

ANTONIA: Where's George?

ROB: Isn't he with you?

ANTONIA: *(Laughing.)* What an idea! I don't think Kay would care for that.

ROB: 'George' would love it. *(ANTONIA laughs.)* Your hubby still in the Bahamas?

ANTIONIA: No, Steve's in Italy. He's doing a documentary for C.B.S. on the Neo Fascists.

ROB: Sit down.

ANTONIA: *(Sitting on the sofa.)* Thanks. Can you smell anything?

ROB: George's burnt dinner.

ANTONIA: Oh.

ROB: Do I make you nervous?

ANTONIA: *(Smiling.)* You are vaguely like your father.

ROB: *(Sitting beside her on the sofa.)* Dad's a fool. He could have you on a plate. Well, he could, couldn't he?

(ANTONIA laughs. KAY comes in with a bottle of milk.)

ANTONIA: Oh, thanks very much, Kay. You've saved my bacon again.

ROB: I'll ring Dad's office.

KAY: Why?

ROB: Just had a premonition.

(ROB exits into the hall.)

ANTONIA: Anything wrong, Kay?

KAY: Has he left you?

(Pause.)

ANTONIA: Who?

KAY: Steve.

ANTONIA: *(Laughing nervously.)* Wow! *(Pointing to a box of chocolates.)* May I…have a chocolate?

KAY: Yes, of course. Don't you want to talk about it?

ANTONIA: *(Biting into a chocolate.)* Ugh! Ginger.

KAY: Got them for Christmas. No one liked them then. *(Taking a chocolate.)* Except me.

ANTONIA: *(Taking a letter from her pocket and giving it to KAY)* This came this morning.

KAY: You want me to read it? *(ANTONIA nods. KAY reads.)* This a joke?

ANTONIA: Yes, I suppose my husband putting his Irish dolly bird in the Club, is pretty funny.

KAY: But it's addressed to you?

ANTONIA: Yes. Obviously the dolly bird asked Steve to cough up for an abortion, but he must've liked the idea of playing father again, so he turned her down. Now she's written to me, to see if I'll finance the operation.

KAY: What perverse cheek!

ANTONIA: Oh, I don't know.

KAY: You can't pay for her abortion! Not that you'd want to.

ANTONIA: Why not?

KAY: Why the hell should you?

ANTONIA: To cut down the Unwanted Kids quota. Every little helps. *(Laughing/crying.)* And unwanted wives. *(KAY hugs her.)* Sorry, Kay, sorry.

KAY: Isn't he coming back, then?

ANTONIA: God knows.

(ROB re-enters.)

ROB: I don't get it.

KAY: Have you found him?

ROB: According to Alf, the doorman; 'At twelve-thirty precisely your father said he was going out to celebrate. When I asked him *what* he was going to celebrate, he said; 'Life, Mr. Todger, life'. Well, you could've knocked me down with a feather, sir. I mean, how can you celebrate anything as horrible as 'Life'?'

KAY: Sounds like your father's had another turn.

ANTONIA: Has he been very depressed, then, recently?

ROB: He can't stop laughing if that's what you mean. Dad only has to hear about a crippling strike, a drop in the Stock Market, or any other 'British disaster', and he's rolling in the aisles.

KAY: Don't exaggerate, dear. He never laughs at Mr. Scanlon or Mr. Scargill. *(Moving to the door.)* And Mr. Tony Benn gives him the positive shakes.

ROB: Where are you...?

KAY: I'm going to ring the Police.

(As she opens the hall door, she is stopped by a MAN'S voice, rendering 'The National Anthem'. The front door bangs. 'The National Anthem' grows more raucous.

A moment later GEORGE HAMPTON, who is handsome, bespectacled and in his mid-Forties, bursts into the room. He is waving a large Union Jack, and carrying a Fortnum and Masons' hamper.

General amazement.

He stops half way through the second verse.)

GEORGE: On your feet, Antonia, for Her Majesty!

KAY: *(Hugging him.)* Thank God. Where the blazes have you been, George? *(GEORGE launches back into 'The National Anthem'. ROB joins in, and GEORGE conducts.)* Stop it George! Both of you, stop it! *(GEORGE stops.)* It's not funny, dear. We've been worried sick.

GEORGE: *(Kissing her on the nose.)* Saint George was quite safe, darling. There are no dragons in Richmond Park.

KAY: Richmond...?

GEORGE: Yes, I dropped in among the stags to celebrate my Sainted namesake's Birthday. It was a wondrous experience. Just me, the trees, the wind and the deer. I even contemplated running naked through the undergrowth waving my banner, but I thought the Park Warden might misconstrue my intentions and have me arrested, so I settled for galloping around Pen Ponds, with my flag fluttering behind me and the swans honking.

KAY: *(Feeling his forehead.)* You're ill, darling.

GEORGE: Soon I was trampling the young ferns as the sun guttered into the treetops. And all the time the mist was oozing up my legs 'till I was waist-deep in white. Then I saw him! Between the silver birch. His heavy antlers like bats' wings against the sunset.

KAY: You've been drinking, haven't you? You've come home stinking-drunk.

GEORGE: *(Breathing on her.)* Smell. Chaste as a nun's armpit.

KAY: You're high as a kite!

GEORGE: *(Opening his hamper.)* If only that were true.

ROB: What...?

GEORGE: Champers, my boy! Caviar. Smoked salmon. And truffles. Otherwise known as a 'Stock Exchange Snack'. Get the glasses out, lad, the Crown Derby. And let us, eat, drink and be merry for tomorrow we snuff it! Hurry, boy. Well, it's not every day you eat like a Peer eats every day.

ROB: *(Getting some glasses.)* Hang around, Dad, I'm doing my best.

KAY: What are we supposed to be celebrating? And don't say 'Life' or I'll scream!

GEORGE: *(Pouring champagne.)* Wine, ho! *(Singing.)*

'And let me the cannakin clink, clink, clink,
And let me the cannakin clink!
A soldier's a man,
A life's but a span,
Why then let a soldier drink!'

(He clinks glasses with KAY.)

KAY: What's all this 'clink, clink, clink'?

GEORGE: *(Now serving canapés.)* Iago's drinking song.

KAY: He's gone off his head.

ROB: It's his birthday, Mum.

KAY: Iago's?

ROB: Shakespeare's.

GEORGE: And Saint George's! *(Swigging his champagne.)* It's the most English day of the whole year. What we need is an

Elizabethan galliard. *(He puts a record on as ANTONIA makes for the door.)* Where d'you think you're off to?

ANTONIA: Sorry, George, but if the twins wake up, they'll be frightened.

GEORGE: *(Passing her a smoked salmon canapé.)* Sit down and munch this.

ANTONIA: I'm a bad enough mother as it is without...

GEORGE: *(Squirting lemon on her smoked salmon.)* Little squirt of lemon. Light the candles, Kay. Flick of Cayenne pepper, and it's a feast for a king! More champers, Rob? *(KAY lights the candles.)* Hmmm...isn't that beautiful?

KAY: Fantastic. Now will you kindly tell us what all this nonsense is about? It must have cost a fortune.

GEORGE: As soon as the stag moved out of the trees, with the orange sun crowning his antlers, suddenly I knew what to do.

ROB: What was that, Dad?

GEORGE: Pointing my flag like a lance, I charged at him!

KAY: You idiot.

ANTONIA: Did the stag run away?

GEORGE: No. He lowered his antlers and stood there, pawing the ground.

(Pause.)

ROB: Go on, the suspense is killing.

GEORGE: Well...just as I was about to slay the dragon, I tripped – and I got a face full of deer-dung!

KAY: What a 'Saint' George.

GEORGE Indeed. When I eventually levered myself out of the excreta, I realised the stag was barely three feet away from me, with white steam chugging out of his nostrils. And you know what? The stag was damned well laughing at me. Yes, laughing. What's England come to, when even the animals get fits of the giggles? It wasn't like that in the old days. Wild boars and unicorns had a sense of respectful decorum.

KAY: Oh, for God's sake, grow up, George!

GEORGE: What a thing to ask of an Englishman.

KAY: Look, we know you left work at twelve-thirty. What we don't know is why, and where you've been since!

GEORGE: *(Savouring his champagne.)* I love bubbly, don't you, Antonia? It's how life should be all the time. Hundreds of bright little bubbles exploding on the palate until one's flying like a hovercraft, skimming over the waves, above everyone and everything, including Lord Bleeding Seagrove!

KAY: A-Hah! So that's it. You've had another whopping great row with your boss.

GEORGE: Do finish off the caviar, Rob. It's genuine Rusky, and it's only three pounds a quarter. *(To KAY.)* What's the matter, my sweet? You're not snuffling your truffles. At least give us a Birthday smile.

KAY: It's not your birthday!

GEORGE: Details, details.

KAY: You're terrible, George.

GEORGE: I know, dear.

KAY: I only have to see you and I want to cry.

GEORGE: That's exactly what I said to the Director of Investments this afternoon.

KAY: That solicitor fellow?

GEORGE: Yes, and Benson should stick to it. Bending the Law's an art form, but it doesn't necessarily include an understanding of the Japanese Stock Market. And, by God, this country needs someone who can understand something. Everywhere you turn – chaos! This morning Austin Morris said their losses are increasing daily because of the engineers' overtime ban. And it's no use the Bank of England throwing its weight behind rescue operations every time a property company runs into liquidity difficulties. Printing more and more money is not the answer to anything. And have you seen today's Financial Times Closing Price Index? It's the lowest it's been for years. I mean, Hell, what *isn't* there to celebrate?

ROB: *(Worried.)* Dad, whatever's come over you?

GEORGE: I'm enjoying myself, d'you mind?

ROB: Nothing you say makes sense.

KAY: You're even worse than usual.

GEORGE: So I had this meeting with Idiot Solicitor Benson, who is mistakenly in charge of Investments. And I told him quite plainly that I was sick of asking his permission as to when to invest and when to sell. But I was even more sick of wasting my time on the Echo System. *(ANTONIA puts her glass down and stands.)* Don't go, Antonia, you'll like this bit.

KAY: Let her be, George. She's not interested, and neither are we.

GEORGE: *(In his cod Kensington voice.)* Surely everyone's 'absolutely fascinated' in the droll workings of the Stock Exchange. It's the barometer of our civilisation. And the 'absolutely fascinating' thing about the Echo System is that we use it to ask the parent-based domicile company, in say, the Virgin Islands, for permission to buy shares in, say, Japanese Itchiaso lawn mowers.

ROB: What's so 'absolutely fascinating' about that?

GEORGE: The catch is; I'm *asking* the Virgin Islands if I can *buy* shares in Itchiaso at the same time as I'm *telling* the Virgin Islands that I've already *bought* the shares in Itchiaso, which I'm asking the Virgin Islands if I can buy.

ANTONIA: George, that sounds vaguely crooked.

GEORGE: Only vaguely? Let's have another bottle on the strength of it. *(Pouring more champagne.)* So after my little tussle with our solicitor, I barged straight into the Wolfsschanze itself, to bestow my fuming advice on Lord 'Herr' Seagrove, Peer of the Realm. And instantly His Lordship said, with his legendary smile… *(In his Lord Peter*

Wimsey accent.) ... 'I understand you've got a spot of trouble with the Nips, dear boy.'

KAY: Stop playing the fool, George. It's very boring.

GEORGE: *(Continuing with his Lord Wimsey take-off.)* 'But it's hardly surprisin', Hampton, 'cause them slant-eyes are breedin' too fast, expandin' too quick and workin' too hard. Still, what else can you expect from a Kamikaze culture? Save hara-kiri, kendo and raw fish.'

KAY: Antonia does not have to sit here and listen to Seagrove's racist waffle.

GEORGE: No, she can leave and listen through the wall. *(Continuing his imitation.)* 'So you see, Hampton, as far as the Stock Market's concerned; only the UK, the US, and the Jerries matter. So who needs Nips, Wogs, Froggies and Greasers? They've no background. And, what's more, they're unstable, unwashed and of very doubtful complexion.'

ROB: For Christ's sake, Dad!

GEORGE: I won't have swearing in this house.

ANTONIA: I've got to go, George, I've really got to...

GEORGE: *(Overriding her.)* First you'll join me in drinking a toast to all Great British Management!

ANTONIA: Huh?

GEORGE: Especially to the wondrous Lord Seagrove – who this afternoon promoted me!

KAY: Oh, darling, darling! That's marvellous news.

GEORGE: Yes, and my new job will require my undivided attention twenty-four hours a day into the unforeseeable future.

ROB: What kind of job is it, Dad?

GEORGE: *(Doing his Lord Wimsey accent.)* 'You see, Hampton, I don't trust the Nips. Never have trusted 'em. So we don't need a Nip market. In fact we haven't got a Nip market. And to prove it, I'm promotin' you to being...FULL-TIME UNEMPLOYED.'

KAY: He fired you?

GEORGE: *(Overly cheerful.)* Don't look so glum, dear. One meets all the best people at the Labour Exchange.

Blackout.

SCENE TWO

Bank Holiday Monday (August 26th) 1974.

Ten o'clock in the morning.

Same setting. The room is empty.

The telephone is ringing in the hall. It stops. The front door bangs.

GEORGE: *(Off.)* Damn and blast!

(GEORGE comes in, sweating, wearing a short-sleeved shirt, grubby slacks, and sandals. He is carrying The Financial Times *and a shopping bag.*

Groaning he switches on the lights, then slumps into an armchair. He flicks through the paper. Then he throws it down, and opens one of the French windows. He stares out. Then he takes off his shirt, registers distaste, removes his glasses, and goes into the hall.

We hear water flushing in the downstairs toilet.

GEORGE returns, drying his torso. He squirts some soda water into a glass, swigs it down, and slumps into a chair. Then he puts on his glasses, groans, and takes them off again. He is cleaning his glasses when ANTONIA appears, with two shopping bags.)

ANTONIA: Oh. I didn't think anyone was in.

GEORGE: How right you are.

ANTONIA: *(Producing a packet from one of her shopping bags.)* Sorry, I didn't knock but...I borrowed some butter yesterday and...well, I hope Kay doesn't mind Anchor. It's all I could get.

GEORGE: She won't notice. What's the matter?

ANTONIA: *(Looking at his torso.)* Never seen you like that before.

GEORGE: Every idol has to fall off its pedestal sometime. *(ANTONIA moves to the door, with her shopping.)* No, don't go. I was about to come over to you.

ANTONIA: Really?

GEORGE: *(Indicating her shopping.)* Put that down, and turn round.

(After a moment's hesitation, she puts her shopping down.)

ANTONIA: OK. *(Bemused she turns round with her back to him.)* What are you going to do?

GEORGE: You'll see. *(GEORGE dips into his shopping bag. He pulls out a party-hat, which he puts on his head, and also a children's blower, plus a small gift-wrapped package. Then he blows hard on the blower. ANTONIA screams and whirls round. He hands her the package.)* Happy Birthday!

ANTONIA: Oh. *(Recovering from the shock.)* Thank you. How'd you guess?

GEORGE: Last month you mentioned you were going to be an old woman of thirty come August Bank Holiday Monday, so I thought I'd get you a little something to alleviate the depression. Open it. It won't bite.

ANTONIA: You shouldn't have. *(She undoes the gift-wrapping, and opens the package. Then she pulls out a pair of sexy red-and-black garters.)* Oooooh!

(She laughs and kisses him on the cheek.)

GEORGE: Hmmm…imagine what I'd've got for a fur coat.

ANTONIA: Shall I try them on?

GEORGE: Can I watch?

ANTONIA: If it'll help.

(They both laugh. Without warning she pulls up her slip. Embarrassed GEORGE turns away.)

GEORGE: Did…Steve remember your birthday?

(ANTONIA shrugs, then she adjusts her dress and sits down.)

ANTONIA: Husbands don't.

GEORGE: I've never forgotten Kay's. Not until this year.

(Suddenly he produces a rat out of his pocket, which he puts on her knee. She screams.)

ANTONIA: Ugh! Get that thing off me, get it off me!

GEORGE: *(Removing the rat and grinning.)* It's not real.

ANTONIA: It's not?

GEORGE: No. Bought it from the kids' Trick shop. Whoops!
(He makes the rat shoot up her skirt.) That's it, Ratty. Straight for the Garden of Eden!

(Panic-stricken ANTONIA jumps onto a chair.)

ANTONIA: Stop it, George, please. I'll scream again, I will!
(GEORGE continues to hold the rat on her upper thigh. In response ANTONIA seizes his wrist, and forces his fingers against her flesh.)
We're too old for all these games, Georgie. They're so uselessly tiring. Especially when you've hit thirty. *(Shaking his head, he removes his hand from her thigh. She gets off the chair, and gently touches his face.)* What am I going to do with you?

GEORGE: *(Breaking away from her.)* Your twins'll be yelling for you.

ANTONIA: *(Shaking her head.)* Mother's got them for a couple of days.

GEORGE: Where's Steve, then?

ANTONIA: He's still living with that Irish dolly-bird he put into the Club.

GEORGE: Didn't he even ring you up to wish you 'Happy Returns'?

ANTONIA: Stop prevaricating, George. *(In an American accent.)* Shit, or get off the pot!

GEORGE: *(Shocked.)* Strike a light!

ANTONIA: That's what comes of being married to a Yankee-doodle film-maker. Look, sweety, it's just as embarrassing for me to say what I feel as it is for you to come to terms with all these puerile sex-games you keep playing. So stop playing them.

GEORGE: *(Shaking his head.)* I'm sorry, Antonia, but it's the only way I can cope. See, I've been out of work now for over four months, and nothing's turned up, so for the last few weeks I've been in such a state that I can barely manage to stagger out of bed before midday… *(Gesturing hopelessly at her.)* …let alone… Then all I do is sit here in my pyjamas, nursing a luke-warm cup of coffee, and staring at this. *(Waving* The Financial Times.*)* And just… staring… Every day doing nothing, believe me, is very exhausting. Yesterday I was in such a bad way, I thought I was pregnant. No, really. I had all the symptoms. Felt bloated, had morning sickness and a great yen for pickled onions. Made me feel quite creative. But sadly it passed in one ginormous belch. And there I was, purged.

ANTONIA: *(Hugging him.)* Oh, you poor darling.

GEORGE: *(Struggling.)* Hey, hey, I'm sorry, but not now!

(She moves in for the big kiss, but he fends her off with The Financial Times.*)*

ANTONIA: You can't keep running away, George.

GEORGE: What else can I do? Now the world's gone crazy.

ANTONIA: George…

GEORGE: *(Overriding her as he reads vehemently from the paper.)* 'Prisoners in prison industries may get Trades Union rates,' says the Home Secretary. So now you have to sexually assault a minor, or mug a pensioner, before they guarantee you a job or your rights.

ANTONIA: For God's sake, stop running!

GEORGE: Talking of which… *(Reading.)* … The railwaymen may settle for a mere 30% rise next week' – when the cost of living has only risen by 15%. Otherwise they'll go on strike again.

ANTONIA: George, just who the bloody hell do you think you're kidding?

GEORGE: *(Dropping the newspaper on top of the garters.)* And yet, thank God, despite everything, we still go on laughing. Mind, we've got good reason.

ANTONIA: *(Shaking her head in disbelief.)* Have you?

GEORGE: Sure. What other nation could lose the greatest Empire the world has ever known, and then have the jam to find oil in the North Sea?

ANTONIA: So what? The oil's already been mortgaged off to cover our horrendous Balance of Payments deficit.

GEORGE: *(Laughing.)* You should leave politics to men, sweetie, it's our province.

ANTONIA: One would never know, judging by the present Global Cock-up.

(Unnoticed by GEORGE, ROB comes in, with his cricket gear.)

GEORGE: But there's always a way out, sweetie.

(GEORGE makes the 'rat' jump towards ANTONIA, who shrieks.)

ROB: So I see.

GEORGE: *(Now deeply embarrassed.)* I seem to have lost...my shirt. *(Dropping the rat.)* Won't be a sec.

(GEORGE goes into the hall. ROB and ANTONIA laugh at GEORGE's retreat.)

ROB: *(Picking up the rat and swinging it by its tail.)* Did he make it?

ANTONIA: Pardon?

ROB: He obviously didn't. *(Giving her the rat.)* Happy Birthday.

ANTONIA: Oh...thank you.

(She discards the rat, and moves to her shopping.)

ROB: Don't go.

ANTONIA: I have to.

ROB: Is Steve back, then?

ANTONIA: No, he's making a documentary on the US Army. But Steve, with all his New Yorker savvy, says it's bullshit.

Then he says most things are bullshit. *(Imitating her husband's American accent.)* 'But as long as they pay me to go on shooting shit, I'll crap with the best of 'em.'

ROB: How could you possibly love such a crude person?

ANTONIA: When you love someone, insanity tends to become a way of life.

ROB: Hm! Whatever we are here in the UK, we're not materialistic like the Yanks.

ANTONIA: No, we're much worse. We hide our greed under a veneer of snide superiority, but inside we're raw with envy.

ROB: Come off it.

ANTONIA: It's a fact, Rob. Since we've lost our Empire, we're totally dependent on ourselves, and the world doesn't owe us a living any more.

ROB: What would you do...if I kissed you?

(GEORGE enters.)

GEORGE: I don't know what she'd do, but I'd knock you down.

ANTONIA: *(Delighted.)* Would you?

GEORGE: Probably.

ANTONIA: Then you'd better kiss me, Rob.

ROB: *(Twiddling his cricket bat, undecided.)* Huh?

ANTONIA: I'm dying to see your Dad in action. Any kind of action.

GEORGE: *(Laughing, to ROB.)* Did you win, son?

ROB: 'Course not. *(In order to sit down, ROB moves the newspaper off the sofa, and sees the red-and-black garters under the paper.)* These yours – 'sweetie'?

ANTONIA: Your Dad bought them for my birthday. *(ROB whistles.)* I offered to slip them on in front of him, but he had another attack of the Puritan squeams.

(ROB laughs as ANTONIA wraps the garters up in the gift-paper and stuffs them down into one of her shopping bags.)

GEORGE: It's not that funny.

ROB: I got my 'A' levels.

GEORGE: You did?

ROB: With a distinction in English.

GEORGE: Fantastic, lad, congratulations!

ANTONIA: *(Hugging ROB.)* Yes, that's really made my birthday, Rob.

ROB: *(Hugging ANTONIA.)* Has it?

GEORGE: You'll be going to University, then?

ROB: Don't think I'll bother.

GEORGE: Why not?

ROB: Who wants to be a teacher?

GEORGE: *I* wouldn't mind.

ROB: What would you teach?

GEORGE: I wouldn't mind *being* anything.

ROB: As long as it's handed to you on a plate. Not that that would be sure fire. You'd only say it was too hot and drop it.

(ROB goes out.)

GEORGE: Rob! *(The front door bangs.)* I think he's jealous.

ANTONIA: Of you?

GEORGE: Of us.

ANTONIA: *(Moving close to him.)* Well, let's give him something to be jealous about, then.

GEORGE: *(Keeping her at arms' length.)* Can't you understand, Antonia? It's not that I don't want you, I do. But the trouble is, I respect you... Even though I do have erotic dreams about you. Last night I woke up with a mouthful of feathers 'cause I savaged the pillow in my sleep. That's why I have to keep you behind Perspex, because if I ever did...well, make love to you, then my whole way of living would turn upside down.

ANTONIA: So why are we waiting?

GEORGE: I've just bloody told you! When we were at war with the Jerries, things were different. If you'd been a WAF then, and I'd found you in my bed, even I wouldn't look a gift horse in the mouth. But at the moment we're not at war.

ANTONIA: Oh, but we are.

GEORGE: Who with, for Heaven's sake?

ANTONIA: Each other.

GEORGE: Look, even if we don't go to...well, to bed, we can still be friends, can't we? I really need a friend, 'cause now I'm so out-of-work that it's like I'm on a slag-heap... Well, this country's in such a godawful mess!

ANTONIA: So what are *you* going to do about it, Georgie?

GEORGE: *(Pouring them both a drink.)* Christ knows. What the hell can we do? Now that we're at the mercy of all those Communist union leaders.

ANTONIA: Oh for, pity's sake, George, just kiss me, will you?

GEORGE: Come on, Antonia, even you must've noticed that since the death of Ernest Bevin, the Marxists have taken over most of the major Unions.

ANTONIA: Yes, but Bevin is history now.

GEORGE: He was still the last *Anti*-Communist General Secretary. And he knew damn well what would happen if our Red friends started typing the Union minutes and tonguing the stamps. And Bevin was right. Communist Union Leaders – like Scargill, Scanlon and McGahey – have suddenly appeared out of nowhere. The Reds are no longer *under* our beds, they're now *in* our beds. And daily those bastards are calling everyone out on their multiple strikes, to make sure the rest of us sweat or freeze in the blackouts!

(KAY, who has been listening in the doorway, claps derisively.)

KAY: Bravo, George, bravo. You really shouldn't encourage him, Antonia. Only makes him worse.

31

ANTONIA: It wasn't my intention.

GEORGE: *(Suddenly cocking his head in the direction of the ceiling.)* Hey-up!

ANTONIA: *(To KAY.)* I brought the butter back.

KAY: Thanks, I'll...

GEORGE: Shush! *(Pointing to the ceiling.)* There's someone walking around up there, and there bloody shouldn't be!

KAY: *(Going into kitchen.)* Really?

ANTONIA: *(Agreeing with GEORGE.)* Yes, there is!

KAY: *(Off.)* I got what purports to be a Sicilian pizza from that Indian shop. Shall I heat it up?

(GEORGE takes an axe out of the drinks' cabinet.)

GEORGE: No! You know I can't bear foreign muck.

ANTONIA: What a place to keep an axe.

KAY: *(Putting her head around the door.)* He always over-reacts to bumps in the night.

GEORGE: SHUSH! *(Pause.)* It's stopped.

(There is a loud thud upstairs.)

KAY: Poor Dracula's fallen out of his coffin.

GEORGE: He's...coming down!

ANTONIA: Hope he's not armed.

KAY: *(Going back into kitchen)* He usually only has his fangs.

(ANTONIA slips behind the hall door - as it opens.

FLORIAN GRUNEWALD enters. He is a handsome German in his early thirties. He dresses with flair, but incongruously he is wearing running shoes. He speaks excellent English, with only the vaguest trace of an accent, and he has Continental charm.)

FLORIAN: *(Extending his hand.)* Ah...you must be Mr. Hampton.

GEORGE: *(About to offer FLORIAN the axe instead of his hand, but realising in time.)* Yes. Who the bloody hell are you?

KAY: *(Poking her head round the kitchen door.)* He's our new lodger, darling.

GEORGE: Our new...?

KAY: He answered my ad in the paper shop.

GEORGE: What ad?

KAY: Did I forget to mention it?

GEORGE: Yes!

FLORIAN: I would have come down sooner to make your acquaintance, Mr. Hampton, but I've only just come back from delivering some Piesporter to Newcastle.

GEORGE: Piesporter?

FLORIAN: Wine. Mrs. Hampton was kind enough to show me my room.

KAY: Spare room, darling.

FLORIAN: I'm afraid I put my head down on your extremely comfortable bed and dropped straight off to sleep.

ANTONIA: *(Now appearing from behind the door.)* And our shouting woke you up?

FLORIAN: *(Startled.)* Sorry! I didn't see you, Miss er...?

ANTONIA: No, I was hiding... I mean...how do you do, Mr. er... ?

FLORIAN: *(Kissing her hand.)* Florian Grunewald, at your service, Miss er...?

ANTONIA: Mrs. Antonia Elkind.

FLORIAN: Mrs. That is a shame.

GEORGE: What kind of name's 'Florian Grunewald' when it's at home?

FLORIAN: No relation to the great painter, I'm afraid.

KAY: *(Seeing GEORGE is nonplussed.)* Mathis Grunewald, George. You know, the one who did that charming picture of Christ covered in brambles, sores and green lice.

FLORIAN: *(Smiling.)* Yes, it's very evocative of the German subconscious. *(Indicating the axe in GEORGE'S hand.)* Were you about to chop some firewood, Mr. Hampton?

GEORGE: *(Hastily putting the axe back in the cabinet.)* Y-Yes, yes. But...I've changed my mind.

KAY: Mr. Grunewald, can I tempt you to join us for a Sicilian Indian Pizza?

FLORIAN: Yes, please. Sounds most cosmopolitan. *(He gallantly opens the door for her. KAY goes into the kitchen.)* You have a very charming wife, Mr. Hampton. And I do like your house. It has good 'vibes'; as the Americans say. The walls are crackling with anticipation.

GEORGE: Really?

FLORIAN: You must forgive me playing with your language, but it is so much more flexible than mine.

GEORGE: Yes, it's true English is not just limited to 'Achtung. Achtung' and 'Es ist Verboten.'

FLORIAN: Nor, may I say, is German. *(Moving to the door.)* Now, if you'll excuse me.

GEORGE: Make yourself at home.

FLORIAN: Thank you, I will.

(FLORIAN runs upstairs.)

GEORGE: *(Under his breath.)* Poncified Kraut.

KAY: *(Re-entering.)* He's paying £15 a week rent, darling.

GEORGE: Who needs it?

KAY: *(Going out.)* We do.

GEORGE: Hm! Wonder what *he* was doing during the war?

ANTONIA: Crapping his nappies, I shouldn't wonder.

GEORGE: No, they were signed up for the Hitler Youth before they could crawl.

ANTONIA: Continentals have such charm.

GEORGE: Give me the Japs any day. 'Least you know where you are with all that inscrutability – being economically screwed. *(ANTONIA moves to the door, with her shopping bags.)* No, stay for some Pizza, Antonia.

ANTONIA: 'Whistle and I Will Come to You, My Lad'.

GEORGE: Eh?

ANTONIA: Title of a ghost story.

GEORGE: Very appropriate.

ANTONIA: And I will.

(ANTONIA goes out through the kitchen. FLORIAN returns with a bottle of wine.)

FLORIAN: One of the perks of the trade.

GEORGE: You make your living selling booze, then?

FLORIAN: *(Nodding.)* Stein wine'll go well with Pizza. *(Removing the cork.)* Mmm…excellent bouquet.

GEORGE: *(Producing glasses.)* You could be the perfect lodger.

FLORIAN: *(Pouring.)* I'll do my best.

GEORGE: There is er…just one thing, Mr. Grunewald?

FLORIAN: What was I doing during the War, Mr Hampton?

GEORGE: How'd you guess?

FLORIAN: *(Amused.)* I was having a love affair.

GEORGE: Come again?

FLORIAN: With my mother's breast. *(Going into kitchen with the wine bottle and a glass.)* Try this, Mrs. Hampton. *(Off.)* I think you'll like it.

GEORGE: *(Looking out of the window.)* That your van out there?

KAY: *(Off.)* Oh, that's absolutely delicious.

FLORIAN: *(Off.)* It's better chilled, but…

GEORGE: Mr. Grunewald, your van is blocking our driveway.

FLORIAN: *(Re-appearing.)* Sorry, Mr Hampton, I'll move it.

(KAY comes in with her glass of wine.)

KAY: There's no need. Since George shouted his way out of his job, we've not been able to afford to run our car.

GEORGE: That doesn't mean we have to have a Kraut... er German van blocking our...

(As the phone rings in the hall, GEORGE trails off.)

KAY: You get it, dear. It's bound to be one of your drinking pals, wanting to commiserate on mutual redundancy.

GEORGE: Damn well hope it is!

(GEORGE charges off into the hall.)

KAY: I'm sorry about that, Mr Grunewald, but...

(GEORGE reappears to pour himself some wine.)

GEORGE: *(With an ironic Nazi salute to FLORIAN.)* Sieg Heil!

(GEORGE exits, with his wine.)

KAY: I'm dreadfully sorry. My husband's not usually so offensive.

FLORIAN: Please don't apologise, Mrs. Hampton. If a man can't be himself in his own castle, where can he be?

KAY: You're not offended?

FLORIAN: *(Smiling.)* No, I sympathise. *(Pouring them both some more wine.)* When you live in a fourth rate, down-at-heel country with national bankruptcy around the corner, it's bound to make you feel frenetically schizoid. My mother said that Father felt much the same way during the Weimar Republic. But then a Leader came along and pulled him up by his bootstraps. Right up.

KAY: You mean Hitler.

FLORIAN: Yes. My father was a Nazi.

KAY: Oh dear.

FLORIAN: Only an itzy-bitzy Nazi. An enthusiastic corporal on the Russian Front.

KAY: Was your father at Stalingrad?

FLORIAN: No, he was killed in the biggest tank battle of all time, July '43. At a little place north of Karkhov, called Kursk. Hitler threw in 17 Panzer Divisions against Uncle

Joe, but Joe had over 3000 tanks. So along with most of his friends, Dad went up in a puff of smoke.

KAY: Oh, I'm sorry. Do *you* sympathise with – with...?

FLORIAN: National Socialism? *(KAY nods. FLORIAN laughs.)* No. I'm one of your new aspiring Social Democrats who is very glad that the Third Reich was lucky enough to be defeated by the Soviets, bombed flat by the British and rebuilt by the Americans. I mean, we could have been in your shoes, God help us, and won the bleeding war!

KAY: *(Agitatedly spilling some of her wine.)* I wouldn't change countries with you for the world.

FLORIAN: Maybe not for the world. Just for our German standard of living and our Balance of Payment Surplus.

KAY: Thanks for the good news.

FLORIAN: No, forgive me, Mrs Hampton. That was churlish of me. But, you see, we Germans are very unlike you British in one crucial way. We don't flirt with the Work Ethic, like you do; we've *married* her. Mind, if you don't start to at least 'embrace' the Work Ethic very soon, your Marxist Union leaders may well force you to 'live in sin' with her forever.

KAY: Oh, you don't believe that we've got Reds under our beds, do you?

FLORIAN: Absolutely. Communism is the greatest evil that's existed on the planet.

KAY: That's an absurd assertion. Hitler was far worse than Stalin!

FLORIAN: Sorry, but you're wrong, Mrs Hampton. Stalin killed 3 times more people than Hitler. He boasted to Churchill at Potsdam that he'd already killed over 10 million peasants.

KAY: Unbelievable.

FLORIAN: And even as we speak, God knows how many millions Mao Tse Tung is killing in China.

KAY: Yes, I suppose we'll never know the truth about China.

FLORIAN: One day we will, and we'll be equally horrified. But despite this, Communism still continues to be dangerously alluring – because it *appears* to offer the opportunity for everyone to be equal. But, in reality, when Marxism controls over a third of the world – as it does now – all you get is totalitarianism and nationalised slavery.

KAY: My God, you're jolly fluent for a... well, aren't you?

FLORIAN: I'm cheating. My mother is English.

KAY: I still don't understand why someone in...well, in the wine-trade should get so worked-up about politics.

FLORIAN: If you were born in Germany, like I was, Mrs Hampton, and you discovered that, despite your horrific Nazi history, that Democracy actually works in your country – which it *does* now in West Germany – then, believe me, you would do everything in your power to ensure that your Democracy survives. And you Brits should be doing the same here, or you could end up on the other side of the Wall.

KAY: Oh come on, our Democracy is as safe as houses.

FLORIAN: Not if you look at your disastrous house-market, it isn't. What's more, it's Prime Minister Wilson, who's responsible for most of your present chaos.

KAY: No, Wilson is doing his level-best to deal with all the strikes. He's always having cups of tea with the Union leaders at Number Ten.

FLORIAN: Of course he is. 'Cause it was Wilson, who allowed the Trades Union Marxists to join the Labour Party in the first place. See, he conveniently forgot Comrade Lenin's infamous dictum.

KAY: What 'infamous dictum' is that?

FLORIAN: *(In his best Russian accent.)* 'British Communists must infiltrate the Labour Party, and support it as the rope supports the hanged man!'

KAY: Lenin really said that?

FLORIAN: Yes, but that's not the worst of it. Now the Labour Party has now gone so far to the Left, it will encourage the Tory Party to move even further to the Right. And this will result in more and more crippling strikes, which will cause even more unemployment. So the result is endless misery for everyone.

KAY: Can you smell that?

FLORIAN: Yes, what is it?

KAY: The pizza!

FLORIAN: I'm sure you've cooked it perfectly to a crisp.

KAY: *(Rushing into kitchen.)* That's what worries me.

(GEORGE comes in from hall.)

GEORGE: Kay! *(Sniffing.)* Heavens, what's happened to the pizza?

KAY: *(Re-entering.)* It's exploded. So, what's new, dear?

GEORGE: Charley thinks he's found me a job.

KAY: Marvellous! Japanese investment?

GEORGE: Charley didn't go into the details. But he's over at *The Sun Inn* waiting for me. Won't be long.

KAY: You will take the job, won't you? Whatever it is.

GEORGE: I'll see.

KAY: You've got to do something, darling. You've been out of work for six months.

GEORGE: Oh, come on, it's only just over four.

KAY: Alright, four. But you're at an age when jobs are increasingly hard to come by. So, George, please take what's offered.

GEORGE: Including Antonia?

KAY: If it'll bring you down to earth, yes.

GEORGE: Oh, Antonia'll give me a lift. *(To FLORIAN.)* Enjoy my wife, Mr. Grunewald. She's very down to earth.

(GEORGE goes.)

FLORIAN: Would you excuse an impertinence?

KAY: *(Smiling.)* As long as it's not political.

FLORIAN: May I call you 'Kay'?

KAY: Of course – Florian. *(Continuing to smile.)* Well?

FLORIAN: When I was passing your…bedroom earlier, I noticed the door was wide open. And I saw something inside – which intrigued me.

KAY: What was it?

FLORIAN: I'll bring it down.

(FLORIAN runs out of the room and up the stairs.)

KAY: Florian. Florian! *(Pause. FLORIAN returns, clutching a large painter's folder)* Oh, that.

FLORIAN: Yes.

KAY: You had no right to pry!

FLORIAN: I know but I couldn't resist peeking inside. *(Flicking through the folder.)* And what I saw disturbed and impressed me. *(Taking out a painting.)* This one for instance, contains the same kind of horror as Hieronymus Bosch.

KAY: Put it away, it's rubbish. How did you manage to find them, anyway?

FLORIAN: I saw them lying on your bed.

KAY: God, how could I have left them there?

FLORIAN: Doesn't your husband like your paintings, then?

KAY: He doesn't know about them. And he'd just say that I've got a diseased imagination.

FLORIAN: Well, you have. But it's also a very creative imagination. The lurid colours, of course, are vaguely reminiscent of vomit, but the composition and draughtsmanship are excellent.

KAY: I wouldn't call the colours vomit. True, there's a predominance of oozy orangey-browns, and that section looks a bit like mucus, but I did have jaundice at the time.

FLORIAN: How would you like it if I found you a job?

KAY: *(Putting the paintings back in the folder.)* What as?

FLORIAN: Rudi Ziegler, a friend of mine – well, his father actually – has recently started selling modern etchings. He's already commissioned several of the more important younger artists to work specifically for his gallery...

KAY: *(Interrupting.)* I couldn't do that. I'm not good enough. I've never done an etching in my life.

FLORIAN: You mistake me. I don't mean that Ziegler would put you under contract. Though I'm sure he would like to have you in his gallery.

KAY: Presumably to nail me on the wall?

FLORIAN: *(Laughing.)* No. He needs an artistic adviser, an assistant. There's certainly a vacancy on his sales-staff. What do you think?

KAY: *(Shaking her head.)* I couldn't. You see, since I left art school, I've rather lost confidence in my judgement. I suppose I've hidden behind George, our marriage...and my son. My nerve has gone, so I no longer trust in my artistic abilities. Look, it's a very generous suggestion, Florian, but I'm sorry.

FLORIAN: I understand. But if I ever can be of help, Kay, don't hesitate to ask. Will you join me in another bottle of wine?

KAY: No. No, thank you.

(KAY starts to cry.)

FLORIAN: Kay, what's the matter?

KAY: I'm being ridiculous, I know. But no one's ever noticed my painting before, and I've been knocking them out now for the last ten years. I've got oils, brushes, turpentine hidden everywhere. The kitchen, bathroom... *(Pointing to the bookshelves.)* Even stashed behind there. I'm a regular painting-dypso. But in all that time neither George nor Rob have ever... And I'm always giving myself away. Yet *you've* only been in the house five minutes.

FLORIAN: Yes, well, I'll er... put them back. I apologise for snooping.

KAY: Don't. It's the best thing that's happened for God knows how long. Even if they do look like vomit.

FLORIAN: They don't, they don't. *(Pulling a painting out of the folder.)* This one in particular is...

KAY: *(Cutting in.)* I know; a snot blotch in a pool of gangrene. *(Pushing the painting back in the folder.)* That's how life seems to me sometimes. Everywhere you turn; the TV, newspapers, radio – full of nothing but pain and violence. That's why my paintings scream with disbelief and exhaustion. If I were a man, I'd...

FLORIAN: What would you do?

KAY: I wouldn't be like George for a start. *(After a pause.)* I feel I'm betraying him. But at least I'd go out and hunt down some work. There's still plenty around if you look for it. Even if it is in a typing pool, or manual labour. I certainly wouldn't sit on my backside dreaming of Antonia.

FLORIAN: *(Touching her arm.)* Please...don't upset yourself.

KAY: I-I'm fine. Well, goodnight, Florian. And thank you.

FLORIAN: *(Kissing her hand.)* Goodnight, then, Kay. And thank you.

KAY: What for?

FLORIAN: Being very un-English and speaking your mind. I'll hide these under your bed, right?

KAY: *(Laughing.)* Don't go.

FLORIAN: I'm afraid I must. Early start tomorrow. Have to fetch some Alsatian wine out of bond. Goodnight. And, remember...any time.

KAY: *(Pointing to his running shoes.)* Why do you wear those?

FLORIAN: I always have a sprint before breakfast.

KAY: So why have you got them on now?

FLORIAN: *(Amused.)* I'm never sure where I'll be having breakfast. *(Taking her painting-folder with him.)* Don't worry, I'm good at hiding things.

(He winks, then goes. KAY sighs as she flashes through the TV channels. Then she switches the sound off, and sobs.

(The front door bangs. KAY pretends to be laughing. GEORGE bursts in.)

GEORGE: What's so funny, honeybunch?

KAY: You are.

GEORGE: You're right for once. I bring great news.

KAY: You got the job?

GEORGE: Indeed I did.

KAY: *(Hugging him.)* Wonderful! What is it? Japanese stocks?

GEORGE: Everything's going to be different now. You can even use the car at the weekends, and you won't have to take in washing 'till after the next Budget.

KAY: Stop being silly, darling. What did Charley offer you?

GEORGE: You'd better start looking for a part-time job, though, to satisfy your inner cravings, and also to pay for the housekeeping.

KAY: Less money, huh?

GEORGE: What's a two thirds drop in salary when England's up against it?

KAY: Two-thirds?

GEORGE: How does thirty-five pounds a week, bring your own sandwiches and stamp your own card, grab you?

KAY: Whatever kind of job is it?

GEORGE: It's at the hub of our great democracy.

KAY: Oh, dear.

GEORGE: What's the matter?

KAY: According to Florian, our democracy's nearly finished.

GEORGE: Who's Florian?

KAY: Our lodger.

GEORGE: On Christian name terms, eh?

KAY: No need to get shirty, dear, he fancies Antonia. Don't you all.

GEORGE: You shouldn't listen to Krauts on Democracy. They've spent most of this century trying to get rid of it.

KAY: But what if Florian's right?

GEORGE: *(Pacing the room.)* In the War it was easy, 'cause the enemy was out there. But now it's with-in! *(Frenziedly pressing his forehead.)* Sometimes I wonder if the enemy is…me! And you, and Robert and Antonia. Everyone in the street…

KAY: Oh, I don't think Antonia's the enemy.

GEORGE: What would you do if I 'had it off' with her? *(KAY laughs.)* I'm being serious! Look, this is no laughing matter.

KAY: Oh, it is. It's the funniest thing you've said since you got drunk before our wedding, and threw up all over the Vicar.

GEORGE: Kay, for Pete's sake, I've asked you a profoundly disturbing question.

KAY: Poor Vicar. Covered in puke from his dog collar to the hem of his skirt. It was terrible. You vomiting up your love like that, all your fear and cowardice. Yet, at the time, strangely I took it for a good sign. A sign that you'd take your life by the scruff of its neck and fight for what you believed in. But no, your vomit was just a gesture. Another V sign for spiritual vertigo.

GEORGE: Are you trying to tell me that you don't love me? And never have?

KAY: No, no. I'm saying that despite you – and *me*, for that matter – because I'm a coward, too – yes, I do love you – very much. But you've got to stop playing at windmills, George, and make a stand. You've got to DO something. Anything. But you've got to do it. And do it now.

GEORGE: *(Pouring himself a stiff Scotch.)* You realise what you're nudging me towards?

KAY: Yes. *(GEORGE drinks.)* Well, go on then; screw her. But don't stop there. Give her something that's truly yours. Some of yourself. And, for both our sakes, when you're… having her, tell her what you really believe about you, about us. About what you're going to do with the rest of your life. But please don't smirk your way through her illusions. The laughing has to stop. It has to!

GEORGE: Oh, Kay, I had no idea, no…

KAY: Though maybe you've already tried it, and it's had no effect?

GEORGE: I haven't, I swear it!

KAY: I believe you.

GEORGE: Oh.

KAY: Don't look so disappointed. There's an easy remedy.

(The doorbell rings.)

GEORGE: It's not her. She always comes round the back way.

KAY: Think you'll find it is.

GEORGE: How do you…?

KAY: Women always know when the sacrifice is ready.

GEORGE: *(Disconcerted.)* Where are you going?

KAY: To bed, dear. *(The bell rings again.)* Don't worry, I trust you – not to make a complete fool of yourself. Well, go on, let her in. Then be the perfect gentleman and escort her home. You never know what can happen under an August moon. Especially in Greece.

GEORGE: Greece?

KAY: Our butcher said he'd like to take me there.

(KAY exits.)

GEORGE: He what?! *(The bell rings again. GEORGE goes to answer it.)* Oh. It is you.

(ANTONIA comes in, with GEORGE.)

ANTONIA: You whistled.

GEORGE: I certainly did not whistle.

ANTONIA: I heard you whistling through the wall. So I came.

GEORGE: Everyone's gone loony!

ANTONIA: Just old fashioned telepathy of lust.

GEORGE: This is quite absurd.

ANTONIA: You ready?

GEORGE: *(Whispering.)* She's guessed.

ANTONIA: Guessed what?

GEORGE: About us.

ANTONIA: *(Laughing.)* Of course she has. She suggested it.

GEORGE: She...? When?

ANTONIA: Oh, she hasn't actually said anything. But we agreed it was for the best. For all of us.

GEORGE: How could you agree if you haven't discussed it?

ANTONIA: Women communicate by silence. Particularly with the up-turned mouth – which men foolishly believe is a smile. We talk to each other of course, but only to cover the tension. See, we're all plugged into a faulty switchboard. That's why we keep electrocuting each other.

GEORGE: I don't understand what you're on about, or what she's on about. And I don't think either of you do, either.

(He pours himself another Scotch.)

ANTONIA: Are you coming back with me? Or are we over before we start?

GEORGE: *(Rampaging around the room.)* God, if my father could see me now, he'd get an attack of piles in his coffin. Thirty years down the pits for his son to come to this. Carbon in his lungs, waist-deep in black sludge to give me the chance in life he never had. And you know his only recreation? To get stinking drunk down the pub come Saturday, and then to stand on top of the bar and challenge Churchill to a duel to the death. *(GEORGE slips into his father's Lancashire accent.)* I can still see him reeling along the counter, slobbering beer into his vest, with coal-dust embedded in his wrinkles, sounding off about Churchill being the Number One Fascist, whose only mission in life was to break the hearts of the workers. He was like a clapped-out old whale, stuffed with harpoons and thrown up on the beach, spewing out his hatred, his despair, his loneliness... *(Laughing/crying.)* Have a peanut. Good for the waistline.

ANTONIA: *(Moving to the door.)* See you around, George.

GEORGE: Where'd you think you're off to?

ANTONIA: Home.

GEORGE: You've got to seduce me first. We can't waste all those electrical smiles that you and Kay have been swapping. We've got to have it 'away' together, or it'll be another blown Bank Holiday, won't it?

ANTONIA: You've just '*had* it away'. You don't need me.

GEORGE: Eh?

ANTONIA: With words. Like a true Englishman, you've fucked the Past, fucked your old Dad, with coal-dust in his wrinkles. You don't need a woman. You only have to smell a memory, and you come like crazy.

GEORGE: *(Moving to the door.)* Excuse me, but I've got to go to the er...

ANTONIA: And, to top it all, he has a weak bladder.

GEORGE: It's just not my year, is it?

(GEORGE rushes out. ANTONIA is about to leave when ROB comes in.)

ROB: Oh, there you are.

ANTONIA: Hi.

ROB: I just rang your bell. I need to talk to you.

ANTONIA: Sure.

ROB: They in bed?

ANTONIA: Your mother is. Your father's in the loo, being creative.

ROB: *(Escorting her to the door.)* Good.

ANTONIA: What d'you want to talk about?

ROB: I think you know.

ANTONIA: *(Amused.)* A chip off the old block, eh?

ROB: *(Opening the door for her.)* Try me.

ANTONIA: I hope you're more persuasive than 'Saint' George.

ROB: So do I.

(They go into the hall.)

ANTONIA: *(Off.)* Night, Georgie.

ROB: *(Off.)* Night, Daddy.

(The front door bangs.)

GEORGE: *(Off.)* Robert. Antonia. *(He comes into the room.)* Rob...? *(Looking around the empty room.)* What the...?

(GEORGE rushes out into the hall, opens the front door, and immediately slams it. Then he whirls back into the room, and he flashes through the TV channels. Still cursing he switches off the TV. He turns on the radio.)

MALE ANNOUNCER'S VOICE: ...Several home-made bombs today were discovered at a public house in Bournemouth. Two men are helping the Police with their enquiries. The Australian government have issued a further condemnation of the French, who, they say, have carried out another nuclear test today in Maurora...

(During the headlines, GEORGE takes out a penknife and draws the blade across his exposed wrist. He does not cut himself, but he repeats the ritual.)

(KAY appears in her nightdress. She switches off the radio.)

KAY: You're not thinking of committing suicide again, are you?

GEORGE: I'll try not to make a mess.

KAY: Doesn't matter. We've got plenty of Vim. *(GEORGE laughs.)* Was the seduction a wash-out?

GEORGE: Wonder how deep you have to gouge...

KAY: It obviously was.

GEORGE: Suppose the best way's just to ram the blade in 'till the blood spurts, count a couple of thousand sheep, and then Bob's your uncle.

KAY: *(Clearing up some dirty glasses.)* You still haven't told me what your new job is.

GEORGE: If I imploded my veins, that would count as *doing* something, wouldn't it? I mean, there's no point in me hacking away if it doesn't count.

KAY: Did she turn you down, or did you chicken out?

GEORGE: I think I'll run amok tomorrow. Break a few things. *(Going off.)* And a few people!

KAY: *(Taking the glasses into the kitchen.)* Can I watch? *(Off.)* I'm off to bed, George. Are you coming?

GEORGE: *(Off.)* In a minute.

KAY: *(Off.)* Don't be all night in the loo, dear.

GEORGE: *(Off.)* I'm doing my best, sweetheart.

(KAY re-appears. She is obviously looking for something.)

KAY: *(Searching.)* Where ever did I put them? *(Calling out to GEORGE.)* Is Rob staying overnight with friends?

GEORGE: *(Off.)* God knows. *(Pause. Crying out in pain.)* Kay!!!

KAY: Yes, dear? *(Finding her reading glasses and her novel.)* Ah! How could I miss 'em?

GEORGE: *(Off, in a trembling voice.)* I've done something, Kay.

KAY: Well, flush it, dear.

GEORGE: *(Off.)* No, something very serious.

KAY: *(Finishing off her wine.)* And what's that, George?

GEORGE: *(Off.)* I've cut my wrists.

KAY: *(Laughing in disbelief.)* You've done what?

GEORGE: *(Off.)* Yes. It's like a Polanski movie in here.

KAY: *(Collecting things for the kitchen.)* Look, stop crying wolf, George. I'm sick of it.

GEORGE: *(Off.)* See… *(In a pain-stricken voice.)* …I was supposed to have started at…the Labour Exchange tomorrow.

KAY: George, you haven't really cut your wrists, have you?

GEORGE: *(Off.)* That was the job…Charley offered me…on Her Majesty's Service…handing out dole to all the other poor out-of-work sods.

(KAY runs into the hall.)

KAY: Oh George! George!

GEORGE: *(Off.)* I'm bleeding like a stuck pig.

KAY: *(Off, pounding on the door.)* Open the door, George! Please, open the door.

GEORGE: *(Off, laughing, despite being in pain.)* The Red Badge… of Courage. What a way to go.

(Sounds of the door opening.)

KAY: *(Off.)* Sweet Jesus! You've done it. You really have.

Blackout.

END OF ACT ONE

ACT TWO

SCENE ONE

Guy Fawkes' Night, 5 November, 1974.

Same setting. Ten o'clock in the evening.

The room is empty. Through the darkened windows, we can see flashes of fireworks.

The back door bangs.

GEORGE: *(Switching lights on in the kitchen.)* Now that's what I call a truly English festival, Florrie.

(FLORIAN, in a tracksuit, comes in, followed by GEORGE.)

FLORIAN: Stop calling me 'Florrie'. Makes me sound like some kind of sauerkraut hausfrau.

GEORGE: *(Amused.)* Sorry, Florrie. *(Calling.)* Kay. Kay? *(Pause.)* Where the hell is she?

FLORIAN: Obviously out.

GEORGE: *(Putting on his slippers.)* You have to admit I have the perfect touch with rockets. Sssooosh!

FLORIAN: It's a pity your milk bottles were pointing the wrong way.

GEORGE: What's a shattered greenhouse between friends?

FLORIAN: Mr. Price doesn't share your sentiments. When he saw the damage you'd done, I thought he'd punch you on the nose.

GEORGE: *(Showing his wrists.)* My scars saved me.

FLORIAN: You didn't actually show him them!

GEORGE: Certainly. I'm very proud of the stitchwork.
(FLORIAN moves to the door.) Where you off to?

FLORIAN: To promote some more fantasies.

GEORGE: Eh?

FLORIAN: I'm going to fetch the wine. *(FLORIAN exits. GEORGE looks out of the windows at the fireworks, and makes accompanying explosive noises. FLORIAN returns with two bottles, glasses and a corkscrew. He watches GEORGE, who is still making firework noises.)* Only an Englishman would celebrate a 250-year-old Spanish Catholic's attempt to blow up the Anglo-Protestant Houses of Parliament.

GEORGE: See that one go…ssshooot! An exploding cosmic rose, with its tail dripping fire through the dark. That's how England is – inside; an Elizabethan dance for poets and pirates. You know we were once regarded as being more flamboyant than the Itais.

FLORIAN: *(Pouring wine for them both.)* You still are 'inside'.

GEORGE: You can mock all you like, Florrie, but our history blazes with shooting stars. Look at our writers, our painters...

FLORIAN: Painters?

GEORGE: Yes. *(Pointing to the repros on the walls.)* Turner and Gainsborough...and Reynolds and...and...Sutherland and...

(GEORGE tails off.)

FLORIAN: Quite. And, of course, in music you have your equivalents to Bach, Beethoven, Mozart, Haydn, Schubert, Schumann, Brahms...

GEORGE: Well, we've got Purcell and Elgar and...Britten... and...and... *(Desperately.)* ...Gilbert and Sullivan.

FLORIAN: ...Wagner, Strauss, Mahler, Bruckner, Stockhausen...

GEORGE: Alright, alright, Florrie, so we're a bit short on rhythm. But who's produced the greatest scientists and philosophers?

FLORIAN: The UK naturally. It goes without saying that Einstein, Teller, Freud, Jung, Kant, Hegel, Schopenhauer, Nietzsche and Wernher Von Braun have all genuine English antecedents.

GEORGE: *(Downing his glass.)* She should be back by now.

FLORIAN: *(Laughing.)* 'Georgie Porgie, pudding and pie; The Englishman who lives in the sky.'

GEORGE: Well, we were great. We had the greatest Empire the world has ever known. And in those days no bloody Kraut dared flout his two-bit morbid musicians and mentally-sick scientists in our faces. *(Helping himself to more wine.)* This stuff tastes like watered-down treacle.

FLORIAN: Let's call up Antonia and have an orgy.

GEORGE: And we'll do it again. We'll make the US sit up, and you Huns come running. A new Cromwell will spring out of our loins. He'll fan the flames of courage and wake the British bulldog.

(During this harangue, FLORIAN calls up ANTONIA on the telephone in the hall.)

FLORIAN: No, you must come over now, Antonia, George is doing his 'Britain is the Hostess with the Mostest' number.

(He hangs up.)

GEORGE: Mock, mock, mock while you can. Enoch will fix you!

FLORIAN: Enoch?

GEORGE: Yes, I've come round to seeing that Powell is the Way and the Light. True, Enoch is a little paranoid about our chocolate brethren, but on the economy and the need for self-discipline, he's absolutely right. Our only hope is that his death's head charisma will pull us out of the pit.

FLORIAN: You sound more German than us Germans.

GEORGE: We're decadent through and through. *(Waving The Times.)* Well, how can a civilisation of our supposed maturity countenance a strike that allows millions of tons of raw sewage to be flushed into the Clyde?

FLORIAN: Your famous Elizabethans lived up to their ruffs in excrement, and they didn't seem to mind.

GEORGE: What, in God's name, are we going to do?

(ANTONIA overhears GEORGE as she comes in via the kitchen.)

ANTONIA: The question is, George, what are *you* going to do?

GEORGE: *(Peering through the curtains.)* It's not like Kay to be late. She generally rings.

ANTONIA: Where is she?

GEORGE: She went for some interview about a job. Didn't give me the details. Said I'd only be disappointed if she drew another blank. *(The front door bangs.)* Thank God. Kay!

(GEORGE runs into the hall.)

ANTONIA: *(To FLORIAN.)* He's in really bad shape, isn't he?

GEORGE: *(Off.)* Oh…it's you, Robert.

FLORIAN: *(To ANTONIA, nodding.)* Next time he might cut someone else's wrists.

GEORGE: *(Returning and talking over his shoulder.)* Why didn't you tell us you were coming back, lad?

(ROB comes in, with a haversack on his back.)

ROB: Hitch-hiked home on the spur. Oh, hi, Antonia. Florian.

ANTONIA: Hi.

FLORIAN: Hello, Robert.

ROB: *(Taking off his haversack.)* Where's Mum?

GEORGE: That's what I'd like to know. How's College?

ROB: Great. *(FLORIAN gives him some wine.)* Thanks, Florian.

FLORIAN: No strikes?

ROB: There are always strikes. But I've been working too hard to let 'em worry me. We've got an incredibly bright Prof for Anglo Saxon.

GEORGE: *(Disturbed.)* You've been working hard?

ROB: The full midnight-oil bit. I've never been so stirred up. I even dream of 'The Green Knight.'

ANTONIA: The Green…?

ROB: And Sir Gawaine, and Beowulf. You were right, Dad. We really were something in those days. All that blood and alliteration in 'The Battle of Maldon'.

FLORIAN: Battle of Maldon?

ROB: *(Relishing the language.)*

"Afresh he struck him, stabbed so swift
The ring braid burst, and in his heart
The ash point stood. But still the lord laughed
As his blood blew its horn into the sun.
The dark day was in decline, but the dying was not done."

ANTONIA: *(Clapping.)* Bravissimo.

GEORGE: Is that what you've been doing with your grant?

ROB: *(Nodding vigorously.)* Great, isn't it?

GEORGE: You're sick in the head, son.

ROB: What?

GEORGE: You've got a chance I never had, and you're not using it.

FLORIAN: He *is.*

GEORGE: No, he's not. He's bloody *working.*

ANTONIA: You should be proud of him.

GEORGE: Proud? He's cramming his head with stuff in his first year when he ought to be out enjoying himself. All my mates who went to Oxbridge, they hadn't time to work, 'cause they were drinking from morning 'til night, and laying the girls in between. By the end of their first term, most of 'em were bow-legged piss-artists.

ROB: Dad, whatever's come over you?

GEORGE: If you don't grab onto your youth, boy, and squeeze out the sap until you're drunk with new experiences, you'll have nothing to dream about when you get older. When there's only phlegm and envy left.

ROB: Sit down, Dad. You're sweating like crazy.

GEORGE: You'd be sweating, too, son, if you'd had a day like mine. 'Cause let me tell you, you really have to exert your intellect when you're handing out Dole to poor bastards who'd give anything to change places with you. The Ministry of Social 'Security'! What a name for the Labour Exchange. Security's the last thing you get.

ANTONIA: But it's very 'social'.

GEORGE: Oh, yes, and you should see all the colours of the rainbow, twitching shoulders together. It's highly inspiring. 'Fact the misery's so grotesque that all I could do was giggle this morning. Yes, there I was, handing over twenty-three quid to this seven-foot, bog-Irish yobbo for him, his missus' and their thirty-one kids, when suddenly I burst out laughing, so I had to be replaced behind the bars. They said I was a stuck-up madman, and if I didn't stop behaving like King Kong, I'd lose my job, and then I'd have to join the dole queue, with all the other idle slobs in the zoo. Well, you must admit, it is pretty droll; the spiritually out-of-work doling-out charity to the physically out-of-work.

ROB: *(Hugging his father.)* Don't, Dad. Please.

GEORGE: I know, when in doubt, Dad milks the self-pity. Oh, don't worry, son, I'll soon get another job. They're always short of dustmen.

ANTONIA: For God's sake!

GEORGE: *(Doing a twee Scottish accent.)* 'An' the raw sewage could certainly do wi' a wee hand in the Clyde.' No, no, really, everyone, I'm fine. *(Moving to the doorway.)* An eyeful of stars will sort me out.

FLORIAN: May I join you?

GEORGE: Sure.

(GEORGE stares at ANTONIA.)

ANTONIA: What's the matter now?

GEORGE: You look ravishing. It isn't fair.

(GEORGE exits.)

ANTONIA: *(Stopping FLORIAN.)* Please don't stir things.

FLORIAN: I'll leave that to you. See you – both.

(FLORIAN exits.)

ROB: Dad gets crazier every day.

(The front door bangs.)

ANTONIA: Losing his self respect doesn't help. If only... *(ROB puts his arms around her.)* Darling.

(They kiss.)

ROB: Missed me? *(ANTONIA smiles.)* Haven't you? *(ANTONIA smiles.)* I see.

ANTONIA: Do you?

ROB: Can I stay the night?

ANTONIA: Of course.

ROB: Haven't you missed me?

ANTONIA: What do you think?

ROB: I don't know. You're so secretive.

ANTONIA: Am I?

ROB: I might as well tell you...I've...well, I've been unfaithful. *(ANTONIA smiles.)* I don't see anything funny about it! *(ANTONIA kisses his nose.)* Don't you want to know the details?

ANTONIA: *(Laughing.)* No.

ROB: Look, I only love you, darling, but... Well, I was a bit drunk...

ANTONIA: How sweet.

ROB: This is serious!

ANTONIA: *(Shaking her head.)* Just natural.

ROB: I want to be faithful. You're the most fantastic thing that's ever happened to me, and yet the first thing I do is... And she had warts.

ANTONIA: Where?!

ROB: Oh, not there! On her hands. It was like being stroked by a couple of hedgehogs. I didn't enjoy it...

ANTONIA: *(Putting a finger over his lips.)* Shush.

ROB: Can't you see if I don't confess what I've done...?

ANTONIA: *(Interrupting.)* You'll have to live with it. See, one of the peculiarities of embarking on a mature relationship, Robert, is you're not supposed to hurt the beloved more than necessary.

ROB: But you'd tell me if *you'd* been unfaithful?

ANTONIA: Would I?

ROB: Have you been? *(She smiles. He shouts at her.)* Who with? *(Pause.)* Dad? The lecherous old sod!

ANTONIA: Does it matter?

ROB: Yes!

ANTONIA: Why?

ROB: Well, it's... it's...

ANTONIA: Yes?

ROB: Just my luck to fall in love with a sexy, married, provocative woman who never gives a straight answer to anything.

ANTONIA: You know I love you. That's all you need to know.

ROB: No, it isn't.

ANTONIA: It is – because I'm divorcing Stephen.

ROB: Oh.

ANTONIA: Then I'll be free.

ROB: *(Emotionless.)* Great.

ANTONIA: *(Amused.)* Like father like son.

ROB: No!

ANTONIA: We'll see.

ROB: *(Taking her in his arms.)* I'm not afraid of committing myself.

ANTONIA: The twins will be very pleased.

ROB: Who's looking after them?

ANTONIA: Steve. And his girlfriend.

ROB: You allow them to have Jemima and Tiffany?

ANTONIA: Yes, but don't worry, I'll ring Steve up and tell him the twins have got a new Dad, who's moving in with me, because he's dying to look after them.

ROB: *(Thrown.)* You...you'd do that!

ANTONIA: *(Laughing.)* One day I might. Oh, stop being so pompously solemn, and enjoy being in love.

ROB: You don't think Dad's guessed, do you? You haven't told him? *(Pause)* You have!

ANTONIA: Of course I haven't. Now, for pity's sake, take me home and give your tongue a rest. Or at least use it more creatively.

(They kiss. There is the sound of the front door opening. They break.

KAY comes in, carrying her artist's folder)

KAY: Rob! Why didn't you let me know you were coming? Hello, Antonia.

ANTONIA: Hello, Kay.

ROB: I'm sorry, Mum. Just got the urge this afternoon.

KAY: So how's everything? Still enjoying College?

ROB: Yes, it's great. *(Pointing to her painting folder.)* What've you got there?

KAY: A secret.

ANTONIA: *(Moving to the door.)* Yes, well, I'd better be going. 'Bye.

ROB: I'll see you out, Antonia, and I'll get you your er ... milk.

ANTONIA: My...? Oh, yes. Don't bother, I'll get it.

(ANTONIA exits, via the kitchen.)

ROB: *(Opening KAY's folder.)* These aren't yours, are they?

KAY: *(Taking the folder off him.)* Have you seen your father?

ROB: He's just gone for a walk.

KAY: *(Concerned.)* You haven't told him, have you?

ROB: Hm?

KAY: About you and Antonia.

ROB: What about me and Antonia?

KAY: It would hurt him.

ROB: How did you find out?

KAY: You certainly didn't get this morning's sudden 'urge' to come home just to see your father and me.

ROB: *I'm* not the only one who's..! *(He trails off as the telephone rings.)* I'll get it.

KAY: Think you'll find it's for me.

(ROB answers the phone in the hall. KAY glances through her folder. ROB returns.)

ROB: It is.

KAY: Male or female?

ROB: Male. But he didn't give his name.

(Smiling KAY goes into the hall. ROB is about to peek in his mother's folder, when he hears the front door. FLORIAN and GEORGE are laughing together.)

GEORGE: *(Off.)* Oh, hello, sweetheart.

KAY: *(Off.)* Be with you in a second, darling.

(GEORGE comes in with FLORIAN as ROB, with his haversack over his shoulder, is about to go out.)

GEORGE: Florrie lapped me round the block twice!

FLORIAN: One has to keep fit in a declining economy.

ROB: Excuse me, Dad, but I have to...

(KAY runs into the room.)

KAY: I've got it. I've got the job!

GEORGE: What job?

KAY: With Zieglers Gallery. Rudi just told me over the phone. I start tomorrow.

GEORGE: Oh.

ROB: That's fantastic, Mum!

KAY: Florian's the one to thank. He set up this evening's interview. *(Hugging FLORIAN.)* I can't tell you how happy I am.

FLORIAN: My pleasure.

GEORGE: *(Touching KAY'S folder.)* You start at this gallery tomorrow, huh?

KAY: Yes. *(He opens the folder.)* No, George, don't!

GEORGE: *(Pulling out a particularly gory painting.)* God Almighty!

KAY: Please, darling.

GEORGE: What a sick imagination.

KAY: *(Snatching the folder and the painting from him.)* Zieglers don't think so. They said I've a great sense of line and composition .

GEORGE: You're not thinking of exhibiting these nightmares?

KAY: *(Putting the painting in the folder.)* No. I'm selling other artists' work. And I'm being paid three thousand a year to do it.

GEORGE: *(Stunned.)* Three thousand?

KAY: Yes, isn't it fabulous, darling? We'll be able to afford to run our car again, and pay off all our bills. In the Spring we might even take a package tour to Greece or somewhere.

ROB: *(Grinning.)* Hope the three of you enjoy it.

KAY: Three?

ROB: You, Dad, and the butcher.

GEORGE: What?

KAY: Aren't you going to congratulate me, dear? We're saved!

GEORGE: Yes... congratulations.

(He hands her a spent firework.)

KAY: What's this?

GEORGE: One of the many rockets that I shot through Bill's greenhouse. Thought you'd like it as a memento.

KAY: I don't...understand.

GEORGE: Well, with your impressive salary, now I'll be able to pay for the damage, won't I?

(He emits a barking laugh.)

KAY: You're angry. Why? Florian did it to help us, darling. Without telling me, he took a couple of my paintings to Ziegler. Florian begged him to take me on because he knew we were in desperate financial straights. Your salary barely covers the food and the mortgage. Stop laughing, will you? Why are you so cross?

GEORGE: *(Still laughing.)* I'm not cross, my love, I'm delirious. I'm on 35 quid a week, having worked my guts out for over 20 years, and you drop into a 65 quid a week number, having never earned a penny since you left Goldsmiths'. All my training, endless nights of research and a string of qualifications as long as your arm; and how do I end up? Handing out Dole to bone-idle darkies. *(Near to tears.)* Well, you have to laugh, or you'd go crazy.

KAY: I'm sorry, George, I didn't realise...

GEORGE: *(Overriding her.)* Oh don't worry, I've never felt better. And to prove it... *(Holding up one of KAY'S paintings.)* ...let's hang this masterpiece over the bed – for extra inspiration.

(He takes her hand.)

KAY: Where are we going?

GEORGE: To see if your good news has affected my virility.

KAY: Now?!

GEORGE: Sure. Well, let's face it, we're all curious.

ROB: Dad...

GEORGE: Even parents do it, you know. *(Waving.)* 'Night, all.

KAY: You're mad! Stark-raving mad.

GEORGE: *(Grinning.)* Probably.

(GEORGE and KAY exit.)

ROB: Wow!

FLORIAN: Yes, it's hardly the act of a rational English gentleman.

ROB: *(Pouring himself some wine.)* What the hell's happening to him? Dad never used to even mention the word 'sex'. Let alone refer to anything that goes on between the legs – back or front. And Enoch Powell was just a maniacal racist. But now Dad can't open his mouth without foaming on about fornication and forcible repatriation.

FLORIAN: Who was it said; 'If you scratch an Englishman, you won't get blood; only pride, prejudice and Puritan perversion'?

ROB: You Jerry bastard!

FLORIAN: No, I think it was a Frenchman.

ROB: What right have you to meddle in our family with your made-up sayings and your endless boasting about the Great German Democracy? 'Cause you've not taken me in, mate. We've got a good Parliamentary system in this country, and the present Labour Government's doing its level best to pull us out of our mess. So we still have the best way of life in the world here. We're still... *(Fighting to express himself, then trailing off.)*...still...

FLORIAN: Oh, don't stop, you're doing so well.

ROB: Why d'you go on living here if you despise us so much?

FLORIAN: Because I happen to love England. But I don't like to watch her disintegrating in such an appalling manner.

ROB: You 'love England'? You don't know what England is.

FLORIAN: What is it, then?

ROB: It's... it's...'This royal throne of kings, this scepter'd isle, This... happy breed of men, this... this...' *(Breaking off.)* Oh, God, God.

FLORIAN: Steady, Robert, steady.

ROB: Like father like son, she said. And she's right.

FLORIAN: You're still young enough to do something about it.

ROB: You don't like Antonia, do you?

FLORIAN: She's mouth-watering.

ROB: You and she've…behind my back, haven't you?

FLORIAN: Robert, please. I'd like us to be friends, but you do have a definite knack of periodically throwing what I can only describe as a 'wobbly'.

ROB: Was she good in bed?

FLORIAN: You English are congenitally suspicious. You spend so much time squinting over your shoulders, wondering what the other fellow's up to, that you never get round to consummating your own life. But then I suppose that's why on every street corner in England, you find someone congratulating someone else for losing at something.

ROB: We should have bombed you lot off the face of the earth.

FLORIAN: We're very pleased you didn't. And when the Foreign Secretary comes to us for his next loan, I'm sure he will be, too.

ROB: *(Attacking FLORIAN.)* You smug, unfeeling, cocky sod!

FLORIAN: *(Defending himself.)* Hey, hey!

(As they struggle, GEORGE appears in his pyjamas.)

GEORGE: Boys, boys, this is not D. Day! Come on, break it up, break it up. *(They stop fighting.)* That's better. Instead of resorting to fisticuffs, Rob, you should be capitalising on our renowned National assets; diplomacy, charm, reserve and irony. Laugh at yourself, son, laugh. And we must listen to our betters … *(Bowing ironically to FLORIAN.)* …and stop living in our glorious past. *(In his cod German accent.)* Yes, instead we will charge into the Future waving our Balance of Payments Deficit as we 'run' on the Pound. *(ROB picks up his rucksack.)* Where are you going?

ROB: You *know* where I'm going, Dad.

(ROB exits.)

FLORIAN: *(Winking.)* You were damned quick up there, George.

(The front door bangs.)

GEORGE: *(Peering though the front window.)* I don't understand him.

FLORIAN: Have another crack at reality. You might find it stimulating.

GEORGE: *(Going into the hall.)* Never gives up, does it?

FLORIAN: What?

GEORGE: *(Returning with his raincoat and his hat.)* The rain.

FLORIAN: You can't go out like that in your pyjamas. The Police'll pick you up as a flasher.

GEORGE: *(Putting on his raincoat.)* A philosopher like you should have been with me, when I was in Japan last year.

FLORIAN: *(Bemused)* Really?

GEORGE: Yes, I went to a Zen Buddhist temple in Kyoto. It had a garden. Well, it wasn't really a garden; just a strip of white sand, raked smooth. Made of fine shells. There were no trees or shrubs. All you can see are twelve stones placed so. *(Illustrating the garden with his hands.)* Then you sit on a wooden bench and look round at the stones. Least I did. According to my Japanese friends, it's quite normal for Europeans to be loosely inquisitive. When you grow bored with looking round, you count the stones – two or three times – because you assume it's some kind of code, or religious game, or perhaps there's an intellectual catch to it. There isn't, of course. After sitting there and gazing round for several minutes, I remember my guide, a Japanese monk, pressuring my shoulder; ' Look into the garden, Mr. Hampton. Blank your mind. Concentrate on that stone in the centre. Then slowly take in more stones without changing your focus. But don't use your mind.' So I went on looking and looking until I was heady with my own silence. Then the headiness passed, and my vision widened – and widened – like an opening cyclorama as I took in

65

more and more stones. After an hour, I could take in seven without moving my eyes.

FLORIAN: *(After a pause.)* So?

GEORGE: The man who discovered this way of looking, apparently took in thirteen stones at one glance.

FLORIAN: But you said there were only twelve?

GEORGE: There are. The thirteenth was himself. He saw himself in among the stones.

FLORIAN: *(Affectionately.)* You're a strange fellow, George.

GEORGE: The experience hurt, Florrie. It was like seeing a slagheap at sunset. Or bomb craters in Berlin.

FLORIAN: *(Moved.)* Indeed.

(GEORGE is going when KAY appears in her nightdress. She has been crying. Impotently GEORGE shakes his head.)

FLORIAN: Kay…are you alright?

KAY: Yes, thank you. Good night.

FLORIAN: Is there anything I can do?

KAY: No. Goodnight.

FLORIAN: *(Reluctant to leave.)* Good night, then. 'Night, George.

(FLORIAN exits.)

GEORGE: I'm sorry, darling.

KAY: Don't be. I needed a damn good cry.

GEORGE: *(Putting his arms around her.)* Things'll be better from now on. No, really. *(Trying a joke.)* 'It's just when you're right down, it's hard to get it right up!' *(KAY is not amused.)* I wanted to, sweetie, I so desperately wanted to show you how much I still love you.

KAY: *(Gently.)* Shush…

GEORGE: I'll find a new job, I promise. I'll make a new start. It'll work out, you'll see.

KAY: Oh, come on, George, you've no intention of changing your job. You like doling out at the Labour Exchange. It gives you that extra something to jibe at.

GEORGE: That's not true, Kay.

KAY: You have the English sickness of the soul, my dear. You love making the best of a bad job, as long as it *is* a bad job.

GEORGE: Oh, come on, you don't believe that.

KAY: Nothing matters to you but laughing and marking time.

GEORGE: *(Pointing to KAY'S paintings.)* As we gurgle under Kay's pictorial slime.

(He laughs at his own rhyme.)

KAY: What would you do if *I* was unfaithful?

GEORGE: Eh?

KAY: The whole works. With the heart as well. With the heart more than anything.

GEORGE: Don't know. Probably kill you. I hope I'd kill you.

KAY: *(Pleased.)* Would you really?

GEORGE: It's the least I could do. Why? Are you planning something?

KAY: Perhaps.

GEORGE: Now, Kay, don't be misled by my apparent calmness. There is an avalanche of chaotic emotions inside me. One wrong note, and before you know where you are, you'll be under six feet of roaring snow. *(Putting on his hat.)* And I'm not laughing.

KAY: It's absolutely pissing down. Your pyjamas'll get soaked.

GEORGE: Think I'll walk along the river to Hampton Court.

(GEORGE exits. KAY smiles. Then she takes a painting out of her folder, and holds it up against the wall, covering the repro Gainsborough. FLORIAN appears, still in his tracksuit.)

FLORIAN: Exquisite.

KAY: Oh!

FLORIAN: Has he wandered off in the rain?

KAY: He's gone to have a chat with Cardinal Wolsey's ghost.

FLORIAN: *(Concerned.)* He wouldn't be stupid enough to try and drown himself, would he?

KAY: Even George is not that dumb. You care about him, don't you?

FLORIAN: Yes, I'm very fond of him. 'Fact the painful irony is that I...well, I look on him as my...best friend. It's just sometimes, I...

KAY: I know. I feel the same way. The very last thing I want is for him to hurt himself. I just wish he'd show me that, well... that he sees himself as he is. And me as I am. And then take some bloody action! *(Looking out of the window.)* But, oh, no...he hasn't even gone down to the river.

FLORIAN: *(Joining her.)* There's no one there.

KAY: He's under the laburnum tree.

FLORIAN: You're imagining things.

KAY: If you're so certain...

(She starts to unzip his tracksuit while she continues to look over his shoulder out of the window...)

Fade to Blackout

SCENE TWO

Shrove Tuesday. February 11, 1975.

Same setting. Twilight.

The walls are now covered with KAY'S lurid paintings. The radio is blaring out to an empty room, and all the lights are on.

FEMALE ANNOUNCER'S VOICE: The time is four o'clock. This is LBC News. The results of the Tory Party Election are due any minute. But first the news of a pay-offer to the Miners of up to £5.32 for Face Workers. Unfortunately this has been turned down, so Mr Scargill says a strike is imminent and... *(Breaking off.)* Now the Tory Election results are coming through. And... yes... Mrs. Margaret Thatcher has an overall win! She has 146 votes. 7 more than she needed... *(GEORGE appears, wearing a flowered pinafore. He is holding a smoking frying pan, with a pancake in it.)* So for the first time in British History, there will be a woman as the leader of a political party ...

GEORGE: *(Switching the radio off.)* That's all we bloody need. *(He tosses the pancake, which lands on the floor.)* Bollocks! *(As he levers it off the carpet, ROB comes in with a glass of milk.)* Thought you'd gone back to University.

ROB: Changed my mind. Hmm. That pancake smells good.

(ROB switches off the central light.)

GEORGE: What did you do that for?

ROB: *(Switching off the standard lamp.)* We're in the middle of the biggest fuel crisis in our history, or hadn't you noticed?

GEORGE: *(Switching the central light back on.)* Let's go down in a flood of light, I say. *(Switching on the standard lamp.)* Where've you been, anyway?

ROB: *(Switching off the central light.)* To church.

GEORGE: *(Switching the central light on again.)* Where?

ROB: *(Giving up on his light-saving endeavours.)* It's Shrove Tuesday.

GEORGE: Yes, Pancake Day.

ROB: *(Drinking his milk.)* Amongst other things.

GEORGE: You've not gone religious all of a sudden, have you?

ROB: I felt the need to be shrived.

GEORGE: Jesus Christ!

ROB: Yes, He was involved. And it was extraordinarily elevating. Confession can be sometimes. At least it's a positive attempt to change. As Antonia says when she's feeling spiritual; 'It's an honest grab at something beyond yourself.' *(Pinching some of the pancake from the frying pan and eating it.)* Mmm...this is damn good. Two would be even better. With a sprinkling of sugar, squirt of lemon and a fork.

(ROB goes into the hall, while GEORGE heads for the kitchen.)

GEORGE: Bloody cheek!

(ROB re-appears with an armful of clothes, two suitcases and a haversack, and he starts to pack.)

GEORGE: *(Off, above frying noises.)* Seen your mother recently?

ROB: She's at the American Embassy, isn't she?

GEORGE: *(Off.)* What the hell's she doing there?

ROB: *(Continuing to pack.)* Perhaps she's emigrating.

GEORGE: *(Off.)* She never tells me anything.

ROB: Are the pancakes ready, Dad? I've got to go.

GEORGE: *(Off.)* I'm doing my level best, son. Remember, it's my first crack at pancakes, and they do have a tendency to stick to the ceiling. Or they land on the floor. A bit like the Stock Exchange.

ROB: *(Pausing in his packing.)* Dad?

GEORGE: *(Off.)* Yes?

ROB: I'm sorry you lost your job at the Labour Exchange.

GEORGE: *(Off.)* Maggy Thatcher won, y'know.

ROB: No, seriously, Dad. It upset me a lot.

GEORGE: *(Appearing with the pancakes, and seeing ROB's suitcases.)* Where are you taking those?

ROB: Out.

GEORGE: Oh. *(Sprinkling sugar on a pancake.)* First get that down you.

ROB: Great. *(With his mouth full.)* You're a born Chef.

GEORGE: Now your mother's revolutionising Art, someone has to wade through Mrs Beaton. Your Mum and Mrs Thatcher have much bigger fish to fry.

ROB: Perhaps Thatcher is what this country needs.

GEORGE: No way. All that Thatcher will do is scream 'Communist' at the Labour Party, so she can move the Tory Party even further to the Right. If that's possible. And this will drive the Labour Party even further to the Left. As a result, the majority of the poor, moderate British people will remain totally unrepresented by *either* Political Party. In the meantime, Maggy's bound to privatise everything with her rampant Free Market Economy, so God knows what kind of world your kids are going to inherit.

ROB: *(Waving his fork.)* Oh c'mon, Dad, Maggy is the embodiment of all your dreams of 'Middle' England. She's Middle-class, handsome, bright, speaks proper, and…

GEORGE: Yes, but she's a…

ROB: …A woman! I know. That's what really rankles, isn't it, Dad?

GEORGE: Don't trample the sugar into the carpet!

ROB: Now be fair. Who'd have thought that the little Princess Elizabeth would have turned into Good Queen Bess? Or Dwarf Victoria into the Empress of India. You have to face it, Dad, England's always been her greatest under the rule of women. Anyway, it's a new chance. Sure, we'll probably blow it. Maggy'll probably blow it. But today for the first time there's hope. The people have ceased to conform. We might even renew ourselves.

GEORGE: Of course we will. We always have. Despite the politicians. Look at our history!

ROB: Can't you see it's the Future that matters, Dad? Not the Past. We've been given the cue to stop sleep-walking, so now we've got to wake up to reality.

(ROB picks up his cases, and opens the door to the hall.)

GEORGE: So where are you taking those?

ROB: Next door.

GEORGE: You're not… Well…

ROB: Spit it out, Dad. It's the future. It'll make you feel clean.

GEORGE: *Me* clean? It's your generation that's sick.

ROB: I'll say it for you, then.

GEORGE: Don't bother.

ROB: I'm moving in with Antonia.

GEORGE: No!

ROB: Yes. Antonia's divorce came through this morning. I was cited as co-respondent.

GEORGE: You? What about philandering Steve, with his Irish tart? He's the one who should be pilloried.

ROB: It was the only way he would agree to the divorce.

GEORGE: You're going to marry her, of course.

ROB: We'll see how things fadge. *(Pointing to KAY'S paintings.)* Did Mum put these up?

GEORGE: With *his* help.

ROB: You mean Florian?

GEORGE: How are you going to provide for Antonia and the twins? You don't sit your degree for another two and a half years.

ROB: Don't freak. Steve's still going to have to pay maintenance for the kids, and, if I have to, I'll get on my bike and find a job. *Any* kind of job. And so will Antonia. Which is a damn sight more than *you'll* ever do!

GEORGE: *(Fingering one of KAY'S vivid paintings.)* Hmmm ... aren't they so serenely decorative?

ROB: You *do* know about your friend Florian, don't you?

GEORGE: They're full of such spiritual 'uplift'. And doesn't this one remind you of the Virgin Mary in a Playtex Stretch Bra?

ROB: Dad, are you telling me you don't know what's going on, or you simply don't *want* to know?

GEORGE: This April your mother's having an exhibition in a snob gallery in Bond Street. In the summer she's due for a Retrospective in Madrid. But then there's no accounting for Dago taste.

ROB: Dad, please. This is important for your peace of mind. If you won't say it, I'll say it for you.

GEORGE: You don't have to. I've seen everything with my own eyes.

ROB: You have? *(GEORGE nods.)* When? *(GEORGE smiles.)* So what are you going to do about it? *(There is a knock on the kitchen door. GEORGE rushes off to answer it.)* Dad, you've got to face the facts. It's Florian who's...

GEORGE: *(Off, and very loudly to drown his son.)* Ah, Mrs. Thatcher. Do come in! What a lovely pink hat.

(ANTONIA, bewildered, holding a glass, comes in with GEORGE.)

ANTONIA: I'm not wearing a hat.

GEORGE: *(In cod American.)* 'Many congratulations on your darling win this afternoon, and I just adore your swinging handbag.' *(Taking the glass from her.)* Milk, Ribena, Gin, Barley Water, Tea or Molasses?

ANTONIA: *(Laughing.)* Milk, please. You get worse and worse.

ROB: Doesn't he.

GEORGE: Well, why aren't you jumping up and down?

ANTONIA: You mean my divorce?

GEORGE: No. The Dawning of The Woman's Epoch. You should be on fire with political enthusiasm, burning your bra in a Right Wing bonfire.

ANTONIA: Oh, do belt up, Georgie. Just 'cause the country's in its usual mess... *(Linking arms with ROB.)* ...it doesn't stop *us* having a new life. And that's what Rob and I intend to have. Don't we, darling?

ROB: Absolutely.

ANTONIA: What's more, we're going to take full responsibility for what we do.

GEORGE: That'll be the day.

ANTONIA: And we won't blame anyone but ourselves if we fail. And we probably will fail. But through our love...

GEORGE: Hm!

ANTONIA: Don't be embarrassed by the word, George, it's too late for that. But through our love, we will change. From now on we're going to be forward-looking. 'Cause I've had my belly-full of the Past.

ROB: Me, too. *(Picking up his suitcases and haversack.)* So I'll take these home now, while you tell Dad about the rest of the facts of life. *His* life.

(ROB exits.)

GEORGE: *(Calling after him.)* She's already told me enough to last 'till Doomsday! *(To ANTONIA.)* So take your new hip philosophy and tell it to the robins.

ANTONIA: I know you don't believe it, but my relationship with Rob could actually work. 'Cause I'm the all-purpose 'bird', who'll try anything if the challenge is there, and Rob is the well-known Barnes eccentric, who always inspires children and dogs with his fluent Anglo Saxon.

GEORGE: If you believe that, you'll believe anything.

ANTONIA: I do. See, I don't care what Rob's obsessions are as long as there's real life in them. As long as we don't ...

GEORGE: ...End up like me?

ANTONIA: Oh George, George.

GEORGE: 'Least you won't come round here, scrounging for milk anymore.

ANTONIA: You stupid, wilful jerk!

GEORGE: Charmed, I'm sure. *(She moves to the door. He goes to her.)* Look, I'm sorry, Antonia. No, I really am.

ANTONIA: Are you?

GEORGE: Yes. Come away with me. Please.

ANTONIA: What?

GEORGE: Come away with me now!

ANTONIA: You've finally gone senile.

GEORGE: Isn't that what you've always wanted?

ANTONIA: People change. *(Pause.)* Why didn't you take me away when you had the chance? When your wife challenged you to?

GEORGE: We could go to Brighton. Have a belated honeymoon.

ANTONIA: Nothing ever sinks into your snowdrift, does it? You keep on building the same old snowman year after year. You never get the message. Even when his pipe drops out and his Union Jack's in the mud, you still persist in trying to stick him back together. When all you have to do, is to let him ooze down the drain. Then dry yourself off, find a job, any kind of job, as long as it involves some effort. Then grab onto your friends while you still have some. Make love to your wife while she's still here. Read, work, live – but stop pretending. Whatever else you do, George, *stop pretending!*

GEORGE: It'd be exhilarating in Brighton. Just you and me, listening to the surf sucking the stones back into the sea. Then if we hold each other, together we can peer into the deep water…down to where it's rich and dark…and us.

ANTONIA: I'm going to be cruel, George. You leave me no choice.

GEORGE: You're turning me down?

ANTONIA: I did the day I knew you were my father.

GEORGE: I beg your pardon?

ANTONIA: Not literally, of course. But I went to see my father at Christmas. It was incredible. He was you. Older, not so good with the games, but the same mindless pride in being English, with the hots for the Past, dreams as big as his head, and enough hypocrisy to start a new religion.

GEORGE: What are you getting at?

ANTONIA: Father-fixation. That was my problem.

GEORGE: You knew this; yet you had the nerve to try to seduce me?

ANTONIA: You should be the first to appreciate the irony. Surely incest's the Englishman's favourite past time. Along with sodomy and necrophilia.

GEORGE: I think you'd better get back to your 'kitchen appliance'.

ANTONIA: That's a nice way to describe your son.

GEORGE: Well, he won't be much more by the time you've plugged him in, switched on his obsessions, and mixed in your own.

ANTONIA: George, once you had two women who loved you, flattered you and generally stripped off whenever you nodded; your wife – and me. But last August you dropped me – from a great height – because I was hot, and you preferred to go on talking. So that only leaves Kay, who, despite all the odds, still loves you.

GEORGE: I think you've said enough.

ANTONIA: You know what I'm going to tell you, don't you?

GEORGE: I don't want to hear it.

ANTONIA: Why?

GEORGE: It's filth!

ANTONIA: Yes, and once the 'filth's' in the open, you'll have to *do* something about it, won't you?

GEORGE: You dirty cow!

ANTONIA: Well, go on, Georgie, say it, say what's breeding that acid in your guts, what's giving you nightmares, what's making you impotent. SAY IT.

GEORGE: Don't make me... Please don't...

ANTONIA: It's your last chance to save your marriage.

GEORGE: You have no right to...

ANTONIA: *(Overriding him.)* I know it goes against the National character, but occasionally even *you* may have to wave your Union Jack for something you believe in.

GEORGE: For God's sake, leave me alone!

ANTONIA: You might as well shout it out loud; 'My wife loves me so much, but she's so destroyed by my smirking gutlessness that every night she creeps into *another* man's bed, so that she can be fucked out of her misery by MY BEST FRIEND.'

(GEORGE lets out a terrible animal cry as he wrenches open the cocktail cabinet.)

ANTONIA: And what's his first reaction? He rushes for the booze. *(GEORGE pulls the axe out from the back of the cabinet.)* Oh, my God!

GEORGE: *(Frighteningly calm.)* As everyone seems to be 'fucking' but me; I thought I'd fucking well chop the fucking laburnum tree down.

ANTONIA: Ahh?

GEORGE: *(Opening the French windows.)* I need something to practice on.

ANTONIA: Y-you're not considering…?

GEORGE: *(Overriding her.)* When she gets back, tap on the window. Then I'll come in and make everyone happy. I'll really provide some 'action'.

(GEORGE goes out through the French windows, taking the key with him.)

ANTONIA: Oh, don't be so childish! *(GEORGE locks the French windows from outside, then disappears.)* Look, I'm sorry, George. The last thing I wanted was for you to go off your head. GEORGE!

(The front door bangs.)

KAY: *(Off.)* George? I'm back. George?

FLORIAN: *(Off.)* He's probably gone to the pub.

KAY: *(Off.)* Mmmm….pancakes!

FLORIAN: *(Coming into the room.)* He might be in the garden.

ANTONIA: No, no…he's not.

(KAY enters.)

KAY: Oh...Antonia.

ANTONIA: George's just...nipped out. For a breath of fresh air.

KAY: Oh. *(Waving her passport.)* Off to the States tomorrow.

ANTONIA: How exciting.

KAY: *(As FLORIAN helps her off with her coat.)* Yes, thanks to darling Florian I've three whole weeks in New York. Zieglers' Manhattan office are laying out the red carpet for me.

ANTONIA: Kay, could I...?

KAY: *(In her own world.)* Here's hoping I sell as much there.

FLORIAN: *(Hanging up KAY'S coat for her.)* You'll have the Americans grovelling at your feet.

KAY: *(Checking her make-up.)* They can keep their grovelling, I only want their cheque books. *(To ANTONIA, who is now peering through the French windows.)* Is anything wrong?

ANTONIA: *(Backing away from the window.)* No, no, it's just... Look, there's something you should...

(The front door bangs.)

KAY: That you, George?

(ROB enters.)

ROB: No, it's me, Mum.

ANTONIA: Kay, I really must talk to you...

ROB: *(Overlapping.)* Did you get your US visa?

KAY: Yes, thank you, dear.

FLORIAN: *I'm* going, too. I need a break.

ROB: I'm sure you do.

(ROB exits, and goes upstairs.)

KAY: *(Putting mascara on her eyelashes.)* Rob! What kind of remark is that?

ANTONIA: Kay, for God's sake, will you stop playing with your face and listen!

KAY: Oh, do you need some milk?

ANTONIA: No, I just need your attention for a moment.

KAY: *(To FLORIAN.)* Finish the packing, will you, darling?

FLORIAN: With pleasure.

ANTONIA: No, you stay here, Florian! What I have to say concerns both of you. All of us. You see...

(Off, there is a cry as ROB falls down several stairs.)

KAY: *(Rushing out into the hall.)* Rob, are you alright?

ROB: *(Off, groaning.)* Just fine and dandy.

KAY: *(Off.)* Where are you taking all those?

ROB: *(Staggering in with a box of books.)* To my new home. *(To ANTONIA.)* Right, sweetheart?

ANTONIA: Please, everyone, listen!

KAY: *(To ROB.)* You're not seriously thinking of moving in with her, are you?

ANTONIA: Kay, for Christ's sake!

ROB: *(Indicating FLORIAN.)* As seriously as you're shacking up with *him*!

KAY: How can you say that? Apologise at once for that slur on Florian's character.

ROB: *(Picking up his books.)* I can't, Mum. I'm too proud of you.

KAY: *(In disbelief.)* Proud?

ROB: Yeah. *(Winking at her.)* I'm sure Florrie screws like a clockwork-orange.

KAY: Robert!

ROB: And I certainly don't blame you for winding him up.

ANTONIA: You're hopeless, you're all hopeless!

ROB: *(Grinning at ANTONIA.)* Well, you share Mum's predilection for youngsters, don't you, old girl. Where you going?

ANTONIA: To lock myself in the loo!

ROB: Don't. You'll miss the climax of the family Love-In.

ANTONIA: And the blood-bath.

(ANTONIA runs up the stairs.)

ROB: What's the matter with everyone? *(Offering a bowl.)* Why don't you have an olive, Mum?

KAY: *(Shaking her head.)* Feel queasy.

ROB: You should feel elated!

KAY: Why?

ROB: How many Mums have the nerve to slough off their middle-class skins and start a new life?

KAY: Don't, dear. You're only making things worse.

ROB: Seriously. I'm very proud of you. I know what it's costing you.

KAY: Do you?

ROB: Yes. Now don't slink off, Florrie. I'm glad for you, too. For *both* of you. Truly. *(To FLORIAN.)* You've done something for Mum that's saved her sanity. You found her a creative job. More important, you love her. And now suddenly, for the first time since I can remember, she's radiant.

KAY: What about your father?

ROB: Tell him it's finished, Mum. Over, kaput. Anything. But get out of here – both of you. Like I'm doing. Make a new life. It's the only hope for you. And for Dad. Only way he'll recover. That's if he ever can. Can't you smell it?

KAY: Burnt pancakes?

ROB: FAILURE! This house stinks of failure. And you know why? Because George courts failure, woos it like a lover. *(Taking his mother's hands.)* Tell him the truth, Kay. Tell him.

KAY: God... God...

FLORIAN: He's right, darling. You must tell George. *(Kissing KAY'S hair.)* Now I'll go up and finish the packing, OK?

(KAY nods as ANTONIA appears, blocking FLORIAN'S way.)

ANTONIA: He's done it.

KAY: Done what?

ANTONIA: Chopped down your laburnum tree.

KAY: George?

(ANTONIA nods.)

FLORIAN: In the pitch dark?

(ANTONIA nods.)

ROB: What's he chopped it down with?

ANTONIA: His axe. I told him, you see.

KAY: Told him what?

ANTONIA: About you and Florian.

FLORIAN: *(Sitting abruptly.)* You did?

(ROB whistles appreciatively.)

KAY: How…did he take it?

ANTONIA: He let out a great roar, and ran into the garden, waving his axe.

KAY: Oh, my God!

ANTONIA: That's what I said.

ROB: Did Dad…say anything else?

ANTONIA: He asked me to knock on the window when you returned.

FLORIAN: Bloody hell!

KAY: *(Peering through the French windows.)* You don't have to knock.

ANTONIA: Hm?

KAY: He knows we're back.

FLORIAN: What's he doing?

KAY: Staring…at the house.

ANTONIA: Where's the…axe?

KAY: Above his head. Glinting in the moonlight.

FLORIAN: *(Joining her by the window.)* He looks like the God of War. Mars. The Anglicised Version.

KAY: This is no time for mythological gags. Can't you see we've the typical, up-tight, Puritan Englishman out there? With Henry the Fifth behind his braces and Oliver Cromwell in his jock strap.

ROB: Mum!

KAY: Well, just look at him. *(FLORIAN laughs.)* I wouldn't smirk if I were you, darling. Unlike you Continentals, an Englishman bottles up all his frustrations for forty years. Then some obliging foreigner plummets his wife and – whoosh-bang! – he charges into his castle, swinging his axe, and he beheads everybody.

FLORIAN: He's coming in.

KAY: Where's the key?

ANTONIA: He's got it.

(FLORIAN runs into the kitchen.)

ROB: Coward!

KAY: What are we going to do?

(FLORIAN returns with a carving knife.)

FLORIAN: Don't worry. I'll disarm him.

KAY: You won't stand a chance. George played rugby for Manchester Grammar School.

FLORIAN: *(Realising.)* You want him to go berserk, don't you?

KAY: Not particularly. Though to see him commit any positive action is almost worth dying for.

ANTONIA: He's here!

(GEORGE unlocks the door, and comes in wielding the axe.)

ROB: Now, steady on. Give me the axe, there's a good Dad.

FLORIAN: Yes, don't do anything hasty, George. It's not English.

ROB: Hand it over, Dad.

(GEORGE brushes ROB aside. He looks semi-deranged.)

GEORGE: *(Too quiet for comfort.)* Hi, everyone.

KAY: George, dear, I...

(GEORGE grabs KAY by the hair.)

GEORGE: Shut up!

FLORIAN: *(Advancing with the knife.)* Take your hands off her.

GEORGE: *(Raising the axe above KAY'S head.)* I said shut up, Florrie.

ROB: Dad, please!

GEORGE: I said silence in court! All of you! *(Pause.)* It's so beautiful out there. The perfect English evening. Half way through winter into an unnatural spring. *(FLORIAN flexes his knife.)* Now don't be rash, Florrie. Put the knife down. Someone could get hurt. *(Indicating KAY.)* DOWN, Florrie.

KAY: Do what he says, for Christ's sake!

(Reluctantly FLORIAN obeys.)

GEORGE: Thank you. My wife and I are most grateful. Aren't we, my dear? *(Smiling.)* Hacking that dead tree into a grave by starlight, with this hatred in my guts, showed me the way. It told me what to do. How to live up to my heritage. You see, for a moment out there, I was quite naked – in my soul. Frenzied and naked, and daubed ceremonially with woad, as I danced with all the others, under a gibbous moon, in a cold ring of stones. I was drunk with the wine from the mistletoe. A star blinked, and went out – as I slammed the sacrificial axe into her breastbone. Oh, I know it was just a flash of reincarnation, of one of the many souls that went into making my failure of a life. Don't relax, Kay.
'Because the best is yet to come.
When the words run out, then you had better run.'
Yes, only an Englishman could turn his jealous despair into a pathetic nursery rhyme. But as I journeyed forward, through what England is, and as I asked myself why I love her so desperately, so ludicrously; then suddenly I knew what to do. *(In his cod French accent.)* If I was French, it would be simple; I'd commit crime passionel in a riot of garlic and vin ordinaire. And if I was German like you,

Florrie... No, don't risk it! I'd have her head off before you touched the knife. That's better. *(In his cod German accent.)* But if I was German like you, Florrie, I'd invoke the phantom of the Führer and get hacking. *(In his own voice.)* What's more, I'd probably enjoy it. Mind, the Americans are even more imaginative with their revenge. *(In his cod American accent.)* The husband generally shoots the family first. Then he takes a dozen high-powered rifles up some bell tower and blasts away at the town's population for the rest of the afternoon. *(In his own voice.)* I even contemplated the time-honoured Japanese remedy... *(In his cod Japanese accent.)* ...a brief Do-It-Yourself Disembowelling on a bamboo mat with a couple of gongs going for atmosphere. *(In his own voice.)* But I tried hara-kiri on the wrists last year. I had to use a whole tin of Vim to clean up after. So I knew the English way was the only way. God help me!

KAY: *(After a pause.)* Wh...what way's that, dear?

GEORGE: You make a bloody great speech – and then you have another drink. *(He puts the axe down and pours himself a large Scotch, which he swigs straight down.)* That's better.

KAY: Oh, no.

GEORGE: Yes, I realise it's disappointing, but I feel too happy for a blood bath, and much too tired to clear up after.

FLORIAN: *(Picking up the axe.)* You mean – you never had any intention of killing us?

GEORGE: Out in the garden it flashed through my mind. But by the time I'd chopped the tree down, I thought, 'What a silly, unEnglish thing to do.' 'Specially as I'm so thrilled for you all.

ANTONIA: Thrilled?

GEORGE: Yes, I think all this newly-discovered love and passion in the family is marvellous. Honestly, Florrie. And if you have any nippers by her, I'd adore to be Godfather. But now she's a full-blown artist, she probably won't find the time.

KAY: Can't you ever stop talking?

GEORGE: It's the only thing I'm good at. Besides cooking, of course. *(Heading for the kitchen.)* Anyone care for a pancake?

ANTONIA: *(Barring his way.)* And that's it, is it? No tragedy? No drama? No ACTION?

GEORGE: *(Laughing.)* What did you expect?

FLORIAN: *(Waving the axe.)* The laughing'll never stop until this bloody country sinks into the Channel!

GEORGE: That's why we're so popular, Florrie. And why the whole world wants to come here.

KAY: George, I'm leaving you. Hasn't that sunk in yet?

GEORGE: You'll be back, dear.

KAY: *(Shaking her head.)* When I walk out of this house, that's it.

FLORIAN: I'm sorry, George. But it's the only way. I'll go up and get our things. We'll spend the night at a hotel.

(FLORIAN goes upstairs.)

KAY: When we come back from the States, we'll collect the rest.

GEORGE: Take a couple of pancakes with you. I can easily wrap 'em up in a napkin.

KAY: *(Whispering.)* Sweetheart, you only have to ask me, and I'll stay. *(Pause.)* Stop me going. Please!

GEORGE: *(Going into the kitchen.)* I'm only the cook, Kay. You're the World Changer.

ANTONIA: For Christ's sake, George, you're losing everything.

GEORGE: *(Off.)* Don't swear in my house. I don't like it. *(Reappearing with eggs and a frying pan.)* Anyone for a crème-de-menthe crepe-suzette?

KAY: You're not funny anymore.

(FLORIAN comes in with two cases.)

FLORIAN: 'Bye, George.

GEORGE: 'Bye, Florrie. Oh, take our car to your hotel. Give me a ring tomorrow before you go, and I'll pick it up from the airport.

FLORIAN: Thanks – but we'll find a cab.

KAY: What are you going to live on, George?

GEORGE: I'll borrow some more from the Bank.

KAY: You're way over-drawn already!

GEORGE: Then I'll open another account somewhere else. That's what Banks are for, isn't it? *(He takes a bottle of crème-de-menthe out of the cabinet and pours himself a glass.)* Last of the Yule Tide Freezo-Mint.

KAY: My poor baby.

GEORGE: Oh, don't worry, sweetie, I'll get by. *(To everyone.)* Despite all the odds, all the logic, all the cynicism; I believe, you see. I believe in England, in me, in the sunsets, the roses, the rain, the mad dogs; all the clichés. Because they're all real, and that's why they're clichés!

KAY: You'll never allow the facts to get in the way of your truth, will you?

GEORGE: *(Kissing her forehead.)* Not this side of hell. God bless you.

KAY: And you, my dear.

(KAY leaves.)

FLORIAN: I love her, George. Just want you to know.

GEORGE: Thanks. Now get out.

(FLORIAN goes. The front door bangs.)

ROB: Dad...

GEORGE: *(Putting ROB'S arm in ANTONIA'S.)* Make her happy, lad. For both of us.

ROB: Come over for some supper.

GEORGE: *(Over-brightly and shaking his head.)* Got to get used to death in the family. It's best alone.

ROB: Dad, please...

GEORGE: Cheer up, boy. This is my idea of masochistic bliss. It's just like the War all over again; up against it. We Brits are best that way. With our backs against the wall in the face of the Blitz Krieg. Glorious. Right, Antonia?

ANTONIA: Wrong, George. That was another England, and that England's dead now. You can rot with it if you like, but we don't have to sit here and watch you. We're going to get on with living, and make a new England while there's still time.

GEORGE: There's always time.

ANTONIA: Not anymore.

(ANTONIA goes. ROB stands, lost.)

GEORGE: Go on, lad. Take her.

ROB: But...

GEORGE: You only get one grab at life, son; and you're already a third of the way through. So get grabbing.

ROB: Thanks, Dad.

(ROB goes. GEORGE fights back his tears, then he starts to laugh.)

GEORGE: 'Oh, to be in England
Now that spring is here...'
No, that's not right. Should be 'April'.
But it'll do. It'll do well enough – for now...

Fade to black.

THE END